PENGUIN BOOKS

EVERYTHING IS OUT OF SYLLABUS

Varun Duggirala is one of the leading conversationalists in the business, personal development and creator landscapes. He co-founded 'The Glitch' in 2009 and has since helped grow it to be one of the leading creative agencies in the country (Global ad Giant WPP acquired it in 2018).

He hosts one of India's most popular business podcasts, 'Advertising Is Dead', and co-hosts one of its most irreverent business podcasts, 'Think Fast'. He shares all that he's learning across work, life, and everything in between on his audio blog 'The Varun Duggi Show' and writes a weekly newsletter *Unschooled*. A propagator of optimizing life for happiness and high performance, he constantly shares his fatherhood and fitness journeys with the world. He is also always open to having a conversation about anything (literally everything)!

ADVANCE PRAISE

'Varun Duggirala is a Renaissance man, able to juggle many passions at once. His energy is infectious and inspiring. I would be happy to follow his instruction manual!'

—Anupama Chopra, film critic and author

'Varun Duggirala delves deep into his innumerous experiences to teach everyone the unspoken fundamentals we were never taught growing up. *Everything Is Out of Syllabus* is a book that I wish schools would actually put into their syllabus!'

—Varun Mayya, CEO and founder, Avalon Meta

'Life is hard, the world is messy, and we all need a helping hand. Well, thank goodness Varun Duggirala wrote *Everything Is Out of Syllabus*. Varun takes one for the team by figuring out life, productivity, the creator economy and how to lead a fulfilled life—and he shares these learnings with us! This book is full of lessons I wish I had learnt 25 years ago—but it's never too late.'

—Amit Verma, writer and podcaster

T0096903

EVERYTHING IS OUT OF SYLLABUS

AN INSTRUCTION MANUAL FOR LIFE & WORK

VARUN DUGGIRALA

FOREWORD BY POOJA DHINGRA

PENGUIN BOOKS

An imprint of Penguin Random House

PENGUIN BOOKS

USA | Canada | UK | Ireland | Australia
New Zealand | India | South Africa | China

Penguin Books is part of the Penguin Random House group of companies
whose addresses can be found at global.penguinrandomhouse.com

Published by Penguin Random House India Pvt. Ltd
4th Floor, Capital Tower 1, MG Road,
Gurugram 122 002, Haryana, India

First published in Penguin Books by Penguin Random House India 2022

10 9 8 7 6 5 4 3 2

ISBN 9780143455028

Typeset in Adobe Garamond Pro by Manipal Technologies Limited, Manipal

www.penguin.co.in

CONTENTS

Foreword
by Pooja Dhingra   vii

Introduction   xi

SECTION 1: START

Start by Flipping the Script on Fear   3

When in Doubt Start with What You Love   10

Consistency Isn't a Prerequisite to Success, Trying Stuff Out Is   14

The Present Holds the Key to the Way Ahead   20

Questions Aren't a Starting Point, They're Markers for
    the Road Ahead   27

SECTION 2: CHOOSE

Luck Gets You through the Door, But It Doesn't Ensure
    You Stay   35

The Gaps in the Wall Help You Scale the Wall   40

It's Not about the Journey or the Destination   46

Make Yourself Multidimensional by Looking Inwards   52

SECTION 3: LEARN

Learning Is So Much More than Education   59

Don't Just Follow Tradition, Learn from It, Question
    It and Evolve It   65

A Pain in the Neck Can Take You Down the Right
       Rabbit Hole   69
Failure Is the Best Teacher If You Actually Pay Attention   74
Boredom and Inspiration Go Hand in Hand   79
Mentorship Isn't a One-Trick Pony   85

SECTION 4: CONNECT

Good Conversations Breed Invaluable Learning   91
Life Is a Series of Negotiations, Not a Competition   99
Happiness, Relationships and Love   103
I Suck at Saying NO! (How Do You Start Saying No?)   111
Have a Stupid Chat   115
Leadership and Partnership: Two Sides of the Same Coin   118

SECTION 5: REFLECT

Learning to Be Self-Aware Is Like Learning to Breathe
       Underwater. It Takes Practice.   127
Be Like Batman   132
Being Fit for Life   136
You Don't Need a Map to Find Joy   141
Tiny Moments of Happiness   145

Bibliography   151
Acknowledgements   155

Foreword

Dear Reader,

Welcome to a world where when nothing makes sense, everything will eventually make sense. Sounds bizarre, right? Let me explain. I used to have a sign in my bedroom as a teenager that read 'everything happens for a reason'. I strongly believed in the fact that everything that was happening to me had a greater purpose behind it, and I met any unsavoury situation with a smile as if to ask the universe: Hey, what are you trying to teach me through this?

After a decade of running a business, writing cookbooks, hosting a popular podcast and learning how to cope with the crazy things entrepreneurship throws your way—I thought I had it all figured out. In March 2020, my baby—Le15 Patisserie—turned 10 years old. For a food business to stay relevant and successful for that long in a hyper-competitive city like Mumbai is no mean feat. I finally let my guard down and told myself I'd figured it all out. The business was profitable, our numbers were great, I was enjoying creating content and finally had a growth plan for Le15 that both excited and scared me. I was ready for the next decade of absolutely crushing it. And then BOOM. The world was hit by a pandemic and everything changed. I found myself in a crisis that I could've never seen coming. I remember reading a Rumi quote that said, 'When I had all the answers, the questions changed.' I felt like I had studied for a French exam and was handed a question paper in Hebrew. Everything was most definitely out of syllabus.

As an entrepreneur you learn how to be resourceful and to, as much as I hate the word, hustle. But I think the quality that helped me the most was grit. After weeks of what felt like darkness and doom, I found the courage to look at life in a different light. This wasn't the path I thought I'd be on, but I was here. I tried to find opportunity in the crisis and I truly learnt what was important to me. I made tough decisions and shut down half of my business; we launched our packaged products and started doing everything differently. Today, I'm a stronger person with so much more confidence in my abilities as an entrepreneur, as a chef, and as a leader.

I met Varun at a conference just before the pandemic and was impressed with everything he'd achieved. Through all of the gloom of 2020, I found a friend I could talk to about the hard things in life, things no one talks about and things certainly no one teaches you how to overcome. During my many long conversations with Varun about life and work I discovered that he was a well of information. His knowledge stems from having critically examined his life, putting it into perspective, and allowing hindsight to be a great teacher. My takeaways from our conversations are quite similar to the lessons he has so generously imparted in this book, which is what makes *Everything Is Out of Syllabus* an excellent read—it's like talking to a person who knows what life is about and what makes it worth living. Like me, Varun is multi-hyphenated and I love that you can't fit him in a box. This helps him see things from many different perspectives, draw unique learnings and have a distinctive voice. These are qualities that can be learnt, but how? Well, for that you must read this book.

I hope you dive in and enjoy every story and lesson that comes your way. I hope you pause, reflect and are able to draw parallels in your own lives. And I hope you're ready to face whatever life throws at you, even if it's out of syllabus!

All my love,
Pooja Dhingra

Introduction

It's the biggest adventure you can have, making up your own life, and it's true for everybody. It's infinite possibility.
Lawrence Kasdan

Let me take you back to when I was five years old. I walked into my classroom and found a series of long, vertically stacked, curved wooden boards that looked like giant over-toasted pieces of bread curved at the edges! Like a very weird food show version of a post-apocalyptic future. At first, I was intrigued. 'Could this be a new kind of slide? If so, where is the ladder?' And then one of the other kids screamed out, 'Why are our sleeping boards standing up?'

Let me first give you some context. Our school made all kindergarten kids take a nap after lunch on these large hardwood boards (the kind most clipboards are made of and not the most comfortable option in hindsight). So, in essence, what was once horizontal was now interestingly vertical. So we all did what any self-respecting five-year-old would do—We started jumping with our tongues out trying to lick the upper part of the board. I jumped once, I jumped twice, until I jumped too high and landed too hard and my teeth bit straight through my tongue. The next thing I knew, I was in the hospital, and my poor parents had come rushing in panic. They found me with half my tongue almost detached from the rest, dangling out of my mouth. The doctors first tried to stick it together with glue (no, it wasn't the kind you keep at home), and when that didn't work, I eventually ended up with a ton of stitches on my tongue to hold the pieces together. That also meant that I couldn't speak for the next three months (and I've been making up for lost time ever since).

If only someone had told me to hold my tongue, figuratively and literally, I wouldn't have had to learn it the hard way. But the way life teaches you things is often messy and out of context. Because in most instances in life, a mess gives you more clarity than anything else.

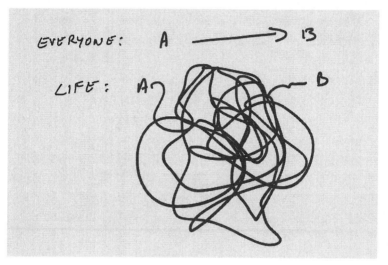

Expectation vs Reality

Speaking of messes, this book is a mess. It's often going to state the obvious, veer towards the ridiculous, and might come close to bordering on pretentious. It can be read front to back or in any order you want to. Basically, it thrives on a lack of order, which is in many ways how I function. It's also full of references and excerpts from stuff people who are far smarter than me in every conceivable way have written. It flows in ways that feel less like a book and more like a conversation. That's because it's meant to flow like life. And life is a conversation that flows in the most convoluted and intriguing way possible.

Life doesn't come with an instruction manual or rule book. Most things are 'out of syllabus'. We aren't taught how to deal with life through a series of pre-prescribed guidelines and textbooks like schools and colleges have tried (and often failed) to teach us for centuries. We learn stuff as other stuff happens to us, provided we pay attention. Life doesn't even come with a map. Life is like a complicated microwave oven you find when you move into a new house. If you use it with the wrong settings, it could set your house on fire, or at best, turn whatever you're trying to make into a half-baked and tangentially different version of what you set out to make. Life is a series of choices made with very few defined guidelines. And that's what makes life fun, exciting, often painful but in equal parts joyous as well. Life is unpredictable and that's the most predictable thing about it.

The idea behind this book isn't to give you instructions or rules to live your life by, neither is it a memoir of an extraordinary life. This book is a collection of incidents, excerpts, insights and moments that have given me some form of clarity as I set out to trace what my life's instruction manual could be. And in reading it, I hope you get some insights into how you can write your own manual for your life.

Let me start with what I began this book with. Four questions that became the foundation of what eventually became twenty-six seemingly tiny instructions that have had the largest impact in my life so far.

'Why is there no rule book for ____?'
'Why did no one tell me how to____?'
'Wait, you mean school doesn't teach you to____?'
'I wish I knew more about ____ when I was ____!'

So, before you get into what my insights are in the chapters to follow, you should fill in as many things in your life that fit into the blanks in those questions.

It's a great way to understand what most of us wish we had understood better at specific instances in our lives. It's also a great way to realize that no school, no university and no teacher can truly prepare you fully for life. Life throws crumbs at you as you move ahead, and it's those crumbs that hold the lessons that lead us to where we can be, if we pay enough attention and follow them.

I've missed many crumbs over my almost forty years of existence on this earth. I have spent as much time rueing the crumbs I missed along the way as I have been grateful for the ones that I managed to spot. And as I sat down to start figuring out how an instruction manual for life would function, I realized a few simple facts. Broadly, there are five things we wish we knew more about before we had to actually face them.

1. How do we start?
2. How do we make choices?
3. How do we learn?
4. How do we connect with those we come across?
5. How do we reflect inwards?

I've looked over my life and tried to compile a list of guard rails for you to map your own life while keeping these five questions in mind. But before we get there, let me first set the context. About me. Because it's important that you know where I've been for you to get more value from what's to come.

A long time ago, in a coastal town with a silent beach called Kakinada, in the year India got colour television, I was beamed down onto this planet. My mom and dad were (and are) way cooler than most parents (a fact that I'm always grateful for but don't say enough, so I'm putting it down in print to compensate). They were also super young when they had me (twenty and twenty-four respectively). I grew up with a healthy mix of Pink Floyd, Michael Bolton and Chiranjeevi (the only actor whose poster I had on my wall *ever*) along with tons of books, love and the opportunity to learn things beyond what everyone around me did. I was encouraged to question things, be as weird as I wanted to be and let my imagination lead me wherever it did. Which often led to me telling complete strangers everything that happened in my house, or speaking my mind a little too often, to everyone's amusement. I also had a knack of performing for a crowd, and so, needless to say, lots of costume changes and drama were a constant feature, often culminating with tongues almost getting cut off or worse. In a nutshell, I grew up around two people who were figuring out life themselves while helping me take baby steps into it, and sharing that journey with them was (and is) something words simply cannot describe.

I was a happy, fun-loving kid living in my own little world with my parents and my truly interesting and smart younger sister (I didn't realize it then, but she's way cooler than I've ever been or can be). I was sheltered just enough from the world to understand how it worked but not feel its repercussions. This changed many years later when I moved to city life in Bengaluru. I was a small-town kid who thought he understood his place in the world, only to realize that the world can smack you in the face and make you question everything. The city brought with it lots of fun, friends and madness but also tons of insecurities, heartbreak, pain and a deep sense of being lost. I scraped through school, lumbered my way through a torturous engineering degree and proceeded to drift through life while trying not to face or understand what my reality was and what my future could be. I didn't just ignore my reality and my feelings, but also ended up hurting and not doing right by my mom, dad and sister. I didn't understand what I was meant to do and didn't want to make the effort to figure out what I truly wanted to do. I fell in love, partied away, lived on a friend's couch, lost a friend to substance abuse and used anyone I could as a crutch for my feelings, only to eventually get my heart broken and keep rolling down the slope of dismay. I was trapped in a hamster wheel of my own creation.

That led me to failure after failure, pain after pain. And in many ways, the lowest I've ever felt as an individual. I took up random jobs while trying to finish my engineering degree which I couldn't for the life of me wrap up. I worked as a promoter for a whisky brand, I sold party cards for another liquor brand, I took up a job at a call centre which required me to work from 2 a.m. to 9 a.m. through the week (more on this later). I was lost and weak in mind, body and spirit. Until I got an opportunity to turn things around.

I ended up in media school studying television production, made friends, found purpose, and went on to intern and work for MTV till I eventually left all that to become an entrepreneur (a term I hadn't fully grasped as a concept when I did). And life found a way to move me more and more towards the light. I continued to have failures, wins and everything else that life threw at me, but I also started to learn from them and grow as a person. I took four steps back but ten steps forward till I found professional success. I failed at relationships and eventually married the love of my life, made new friends, rediscovered family, became a father and felt the purest form of love I have ever felt. But on the way, I even had what I like to call a midlife crisis.

I have had and still have a regular life.

All of us have these journeys in our lives—periods and inflection points both large and small, where, in that moment, we don't know where to begin or what to do. We struggle to figure out how to deal with the situation at hand, and later, in hindsight, we try to ascertain what we could have or should have done, or even understand why things went the way they did.

It's like you've walked into a maths exam you've prepared for, only to realize it's a history test. That is life every day!

So, what is this book about again?

It is a series of insights into how we can start, make choices, learn, connect with others and reflect on life. Things that have led me from my early days as a small-town kid, to the dark ages in my teens and early twenties, to discovering my purpose, becoming an entrepreneur, finding success and true relationships, love, friendship and so much more. Learnings I've had from seemingly innocuous incidents, excerpts and quotes that have given me clarity, mental models and frameworks that I've used to make sense of things and moments that seemed random on the surface but in reality made me look at life from a whole new perspective. We will begin by understanding how to start things in life (and overcoming the hurdles along the way). Then we will move to how we can make choices at every juncture, leading into how we can build systems to learn, and then closing with how we can connect with the people around us and reflect inwards to understand ourselves better. This book is me giving you my instruction manual for life, work and everything in between so you can start writing your own.

'Life is like a jigsaw puzzle; Not a "Box of chocolate[s]". You have to put the pieces together to get the "real" picture.'
Andrea L'Artiste

START

'DO WHAT YOU CAN'T!'

Casey Neistat

Start by Flipping the Script on Fear

Imagine you're an eight-year-old boy. You're getting ready for your big performance on stage in a school costume contest, or as they also called it, a 'fancy dress competition' (I've never understood that name but I guess it just made it sound fancy). All the kids will be there, all the parents, pretty much anyone and everyone. You're all dressed up as a weird, dorky village boy and have prepped for a monologue performance that's going to leave everyone in splits. It's going to be the highlight of your year as you get on stage with all the lights, and you're imagining yourself striding off in a sea of applause and laughs. 'Chimpu the superstar!' (Yep, that's my pet name.)

What happens though is a little different!

You walk on stage, see everyone and freeze. You can't say a word, you can't move. All you can say is, 'Mommy, I don't want to!' And run off the stage in tears. And you can't make yourself get back on stage at all for the next twenty-odd years.

That boy was me! I didn't just choke on stage in front of a large set of people, but I also choked so badly that I couldn't get myself to risk being in that position again for a very long time.

It's stuff like these that make most of us suck at beginning things.

We sit around for days and weeks, even months and years, 'preparing' ourselves for the day we're going to actually start. It's called 'procrastination', but we don't like using that word! (More on that in a bit.)

We do this because we fear that we'll either realize we actually won't like doing the thing we've built our dreams around, or worse, end up as public failures. The second one more than the first is what really pulls us back. And as we grow older and fail more (as we're bound to), the longer we tend to procrastinate and often run away from even trying in the first place.

Because what is procrastination? To a large extent, it is simply our mind telling us not to take on the task at hand but rather focus on something harmless, less risky or something that's comfortable (it's like the four social media notifications you've checked since you started reading this chapter).

Procrastination has a bad rep. It is also the comfort zone that, if used in the right way, can lead to some amazing ideas, hobbies and side hustles that have the potential to become stuff you end up doing for life. But procrastination that's just us escaping doing what we really should be doing is basically fear in disguise.

Our mind likes us to play safe, and if we let it have its way, we'll go through life not facing failure the way we should. Because failure shouldn't make you run away from trying something; it should teach you how to do it better the next time. When you know what can go wrong, you can make sure you try the other scenarios or variations that can be right. The more you try, the more you refine your craft. And what do you have to lose?

In other words, what's the worst that can happen?

This is when we need to embrace our inner child, the kid who, before that first big failure, had a beginner's mindset. A mind that didn't have the 'experience' that guides us towards how we act and react to every scenario in life. Because let's admit it: when you have a frame of reference, you fall back on what might be deemed safe amongst the options you've heard of or come across in life. But if you have no clue, then you have infinite possibilities.

If your mind is empty, it is always ready for anything, it is open to everything. In the beginner's mind there are many possibilities, but in the expert's mind there are few.
                                                    Shunryu Suzuki

It's like our mind starts off as a blank canvas, moves to connect the dots, eventually tells us to colour within the lines, and then progresses to tell us which colour fills which part of the colouring book that becomes our foundational mental instinct in every scenario.

And that's why the line 'What's the worst that can happen?' can mean different things to different people.

This line, in many ways, changed the way I looked at everything I feared I would fail at. It was the single question that helped me decide to quit my job in the peak of the recession in 2009 to start a company with my best friend.

Now, let me give you some context. Rohit and I were three/four years into our careers in television. He had been directing promos and advertisements for 'Channel [V]', the music channel, and I had been producing and directing reality TV shows, initially for MTV and then for Channel [V]. We'd just hit that point when we were sitting at the table and not relegated to being the kids slouching at the back. We had in many ways, to quote what people say, 'done the hard part'.

But as fate would have it, Channel [V] was going through a revamp and was moving from being a music channel to a 'youth general entertainment channel'. A term which I cannot for the life of me understand, because the whole point of creating content for young people is to not make it general or term it 'youth-focused' (call me a youth and I'll run in the opposite direction). In hindsight, this was an inflection point. The Internet was starting to become the space to which an entire generation was moving for the kind of content they wanted. But back to the point. No more music! For the media world, music was slowly becoming a digital thing rather than a part of the television space. Which to our minds signalled, 'That seems to be where the fun stuff is happening, let's go do that!'

'That seems like more fun' was literally our reason to quit our jobs a year after the worst financial crisis the world had seen, and at a point where we were actually becoming the guys who were 'rising up the ranks' in our small pond in the media world. But 'fun' was what we believed in—content that wasn't run-of-the-mill, that would raise people's eyebrows and bring a smile to their faces as their eyes widened.

Everyone told us it was a mistake, that we didn't have the experience or the bank balance, and that there couldn't have been a worse time to start a creative services company. When people were worried they'd lose their jobs, there we were giving up ours to try something 'fun'.

What didn't help was the fact that we spent six months thinking of the name! So, with two months left for our jobs to end and with no actual business plan (we didn't even know what that was) or even a broad-strokes understanding of how we'd make money, we sat down and did the only thing that seemed obvious to us from our limited experience.

Jot down the most obvious questions we needed to answer and the questions that focused on the worst-case scenario.

- What kind of work were we trying to do?
- What were our individual skill sets and what kind of work could those skills deliver?
- Who would give us work?
- How long could we survive with only the money we had between us?
- What would we do if we couldn't figure out how to do this?
- What's the worst that could happen?

And while this might seem like an exercise in 'Entrepreneurial Kindergarten', it was the bare-bones manifesto that kept us running for the first couple of years of our business (we didn't even call it a business then). It was our beginner's minds telling us what we could do, what we could face and the choices we might have to make.

It still feels a lot simpler than most terminology used in business plans I've come across over the years. In essence, what we had worked out was:

- What kind of work were we trying to do: *That fun stuff that started the whole idea*
- What were our individual skill sets and what kind of work could those skills deliver: *The stuff that could pay the bills*
- Who would give us work: *Who was our customer?*
- How long could we survive with only the money we had between us: *Burn rate or cash flow; pay the bills with a little extra for a rainy day*
- What would we do if we couldn't figure out how to do this: *Contingency plan*
- What's the worst that could happen?

We weren't caught up in jargon or the need for 'experienced know-how'. We worked on it like any other problem we needed to solve, looked at it with a mixture of knowledge we had from our careers so far and the gut instinct that told our minds that our decision was right. We had the beginner's mindset of not having any preconceived notions of how to start a company and no burden of expectations from those around us. We could truly just get into it with a sense of learning and discovery, paired with base level logic. Since it wasn't familiar to us, we didn't suffer from the 'Einstellung effect', which is when people default to familiar ways of doing things instead of searching for a more unique way of solving a problem at hand.

Once you have these basics mapped out, you're looking at a frying pan you can visualize, rather than the fire you have no idea about. And that helped us work out the worst-case scenario: 'We'll have to shut shop and find jobs again.'

Worst-Case Scenario

Now pick any disaster movie.

It's always a series of clichés of the worst possible things that can happen:

- Aliens attack—check.
- Giant waves engulf the earth—check.
- An asteroid is on a collision course with the earth—check.
- *Justice League* goes into a reshoot midway through its filming and turns out to be the worst movie ever made—super check (thank you, Snyder Cut)!

But in all those scenarios, there is ultimately always a way out. And in most cases, it's either improvised or dumb luck, and most entrepreneurial ventures as well as career and life choices rely heavily on both.

So why do we fear failing so much? Or rather, how do we make failure our ally?

The solution I found for myself over the years is a simple switching of my mental flow.

We normally spend hours fearing and overanalysing our potential failure, then try to do things in the safest way possible. And then we end up failing because we either took too long or were so focused on the fear that we did the worst possible job we could.

What if we first think of the worst we may end up doing, give ourselves a finite period of time to actually prepare for the worst (to minimize your losses) and actually do the task at hand, and take hours, days or weeks making it better along the way?

Because not doing something is worse than failing at it.

If you jump off a cliff with only the materials to stitch a parachute, you need to figure out how far the drop is and find enough safety gear to protect yourself from the potential fall. The fear you feel as you're dropping makes you figure out a way to stitch faster and prepare better the next time. As you keep jumping off and falling down, you learn what to guard, what to let loose and how fast a parachute stitcher you need to be!

So:

- Embrace a beginner's mindset.
- Work out your worst-case scenario and the stuff around it.
- Flip the script on failure and make it your ally.

Think of the thing that you've been procrastinating doing for a while and write it down.

What's the worst that can happen?

When in Doubt Start with What You Love

Creativity is the ability to believe in the way in which you see the world so much that you actually create an art form out of it.

Dan Mace

We are all born with a natural ability to do things. They might be stupid things, random things, things that don't make sense but that can, over time, create true value nonetheless. And while in life you do build skills to accomplish your goals, to find things that you can truly excel at, often you have to do many things before you find that one thing that sparks what is uniquely 'you'.

Tapping into that which only we can do, and finding a way to not just leverage it for professional success but personal satisfaction as well, is a feeling like no other. But let's be honest. We mostly ignore what comes naturally to us, let it go into that box of 'stuff' we can do as hobbies or just for fun.

I remember as a kid I would come up with imaginary stories in every situation. Climbing the tiled roof of the house I grew up in was me scaling a mountain, and a walk along the beach was a treasure hunt. During my playtime with my toys, I created stories, twists, arcs and resounding climaxes (which included, to my mother's horror, red paint on action figures to make the action realistic). This

10

habit would occasionally pop up when I was bored or zoned out, like when I imagined a boring professor was in a diaper while he was teaching me. It did, however, fade over time. The same goes for my need to remember the most random facts and trivia. Ask me about a song, an album, a movie or a TV show and I might just have something random to add. The more random the trivia, the happier it made (makes) me.

As you set out to be what you want to be and learn what you need to learn to be successful in life, start with what comes naturally to you and build on top of it. And when the other stuff (that you end up learning and doing to move ahead in your career and life) takes prominence, never let go of what is innately 'you'. Gay Hendricks in his book *The Big Leap* puts it beautifully when he says, 'The goal in life is not to attain some imaginary ideal; it is to find and fully use our own gifts.'

Zone of Genius

In the book, Hendricks talks of a concept called 'the zone of genius'. In a broad sense, he says that all of us have four zones in us: the zone of incompetence, the zone of competence, the zone of excellence and the zone of genius. The zone of incompetence is everything we are incompetent at or lack any form of knowledge or skill in (this helps us figure out areas in which we need someone else's help). The zone of competence includes all the skills we are competent at, but which are also common enough that most people in our space are competent at them too. So it doesn't really build a key differentiator for us, but instead just ensures we're not disadvantaged. The zone of excellence builds on the skills we've spent time and effort in mastering—things we have grown to excel at and which help us find success in our endeavours in life (most successful people have found success through excelling in the things that make up their zone of excellence). And then comes the zone of genius.

Our zone of genius includes all the things that come naturally to us, stuff we could innately do since we were tiny, blubbering kids. For me it was always conversations. I was driven by things I had learnt and wanted to share them with a big pinch of imagination to make them more interesting or exciting. Even when there was no one around, I would often talk to myself and laugh when something random amused me to no end (yeah, I'm that guy who randomly laughs by himself because he sees a funny meme). And in many ways, it kept coming to my aid in my lowest or most solitary times. It gave me satisfaction because I was being 'me'. And while I built my skill sets, first as a content producer and later as an entrepreneur, it was when I started sharing what was innately in my mind as a podcaster that the buzz came back in me (I guess I was a born podcaster). So, while the highs of being an entrepreneur have been deeply exciting, fun and amazing to say the least, it was happiness driven by something I had learnt over time; on the other hand, my knack at conversations was innately me. And when they started coexisting, it was magic.

But what if you can't find what is innately you? What if that vision is not clear in your mind? Then start with what you enjoy. What would you do for no money just because you enjoy it? Make sure you spend enough time doing that. It could be a tiny part of your day, but over time it may just spark your genius and show you how you can excel further in your zone of excellence in your own unique way. And if you still can't figure it out:

Start copying what you love. Copy copy copy copy. At the end of the copy you will find yourself.

Yohji Yamamoto

We are a distilled version of what we love, and so dig into that a little bit. Treat it like a treasure hunt, where the entire route is filled with things you enjoy doing and the pay-off is the inner you. The trick is to start with what you naturally enjoy and couple it with what you have genuinely learnt, and your genius will reveal itself to you and help you find the unique game changer inside you.

Start with what you love.

Consistency Isn't a Prerequisite to Success, Trying Stuff Out Is

Let me tell you a story.

There once lived a turtle and a rabbit. BFFs who'd grown up next door to each other.

The rabbit was fun, outgoing and razor-focused on anything he put his mind to. If he told his mom that he would take up something to learn or a sport to play, he'd dive in and not look back till he had mastered it. He was sure about what he wanted to do and learn, and what he wasn't interested in. This made him super confident and also super reliable in most people's eyes, especially when it came to things he had mastered. He was great at maths; he ran and won many races. He could also debate many a topic with total expertise with those around him.

Then came the turtle. He was what many called a procrastinator, someone who would drift from one thing to another, try things out and not really pursue them if he felt even an ounce of disinterest. He also took ages to decide to do anything. He wanted to be sure before he started and constantly questioned why he had to. He'd tried tennis, water polo, ancient history, astronomy and even being an apprentice chef for exactly half a day. But once he zoned out, he was out of it. People had gotten used to his ways, and so they didn't take his interest in anything seriously and tried their best not to rely on him.

Then one day, in the middle of a silly argument, the rabbit and the turtle decided to compete with each other in a race.

Now I know you're thinking, 'This whole thing has led to the story that we've all heard for ages. We know the turtle won, yawn!' But I urge you to hang on, because this version is a little different.

It was Mother's Day, and both the rabbit and the turtle decided to get their moms a bouquet of flowers. What started as a silly statement from the rabbit that 'I will have given my mom the flowers while you're still deciding which florist to go to!' became 'Why don't we make a race out of it and see?'

And that's how we came to where we are.

The race started and the rabbit ran towards the best florist in the forest. The turtle walked around like he was in no hurry; he actually kept stopping at every bush and patch of shrubs he spotted along his way. The rabbit didn't look anywhere but where he needed to reach and maintained a steady pace, having already calculated how long he would take to reach the florist. He had mastered the art of mapping his moves to perfection and peak efficiency. The turtle decided to take a walk along the lake next to his house, a route that was not easy to walk through and was generally a lot longer than any other route if trying to go to any of the stores. He took a pause and looked out at the lake as the rabbit picked up his flowers and turned to head back home. Now the turtle was just walking around the lake, almost like he had forgotten to get to the florist in the first place. Ten minutes later, the rabbit had just about reached his house when he saw something that made him stop.

The turtle was standing outside his gate with a basket full of a wide assortment of flowers. The rabbit looked at the basket and the bouquet of roses he'd bought for his mom (his mom loves roses so that's what he got her).

'How?' the astonished rabbit asked the turtle.

'While you went straight to the florist, I just hopped around to all the places I've seen flowers grow over the years. Places just around the corner from home but off the beaten track. It's not the most standard or straightforward way to do it, but it got the job done in its own unique way. Nice roses, by the way.'

The rabbit looked at the turtle and smiled. Then they both laughed and hugged.

'Maybe being a drifter isn't that bad after all,' said the rabbit.

'You should try it sometime, it's the best,' replied the turtle.

Like the turtle, if I had to list out the number of things I have tried to learn and lost interest in or zoned out of in my almost forty years of existence, that list would be bizarrely long.

I've tried playing all kinds of sports (tennis, cricket, karate, swimming and even Kho Kho, which I was surprisingly decent at). I tried pursuing many areas of study and opportunities as a career. I worked as everything from a mechanical engineer, a call centre executive to a promoter for a whisky, not to mention my forgettable stint as a wannabe model. But nothing ever made me feel, 'This is what I want to do for the foreseeable future!'

I know I'm not the only one who goes through this. There are so many of us who are like the turtle and we're asked to be more like the rabbit. That we need to be more focused, more consistent and just follow the path we've set for ourselves. But we're turtles! We like to experiment, try stuff out, fail and move on if we don't feel it's worth the time and effort of failing again. The fact that rabbits are awesome too is something I totally subscribe to, but that doesn't mean the turtle is automatically the less effective option; it's just a different option. This very need to be rabbits makes us wonder whether we'll succeed at anything. How society looks at people like us doesn't help either. But what they miss is that dabbling in many things is as important as specializing in a few.

Sometimes it feels like everybody wants you to stay right where you are. Everybody's always looking for a definition, a classification, a rule. They want to pin you down so they can understand you. They want you to make it easy for them. They want you to walk in a straight line. I say walk your own line.

Justin Timberlake (from the book Two Beats Ahead)

I'm often reminded of a workshop I conducted for a bunch of students way back in 2012. As I was entering their classroom, the professor turned to me and said, 'Can you please explain to these kids that to succeed, they'll have to find one area to focus on and go deep? They want to do too many things instead of being good at one thing.'

I nodded, entered the classroom and asked all the students, 'Let's start with this: What all do you want to do and learn?'

I proceeded to make them list everything down on a sheet of paper. A couple of hands popped up quickly, and some just sat endlessly writing. After five minutes, I asked the students to find two things (could be more or less) that they'd want to learn a little more about and two things (could be more or less) they wanted to try just for fun and didn't really think they'd try a second time if they didn't like it. Then I told them to make three circles, putting the deeper ones in the circle on the left and the fun try-once-if-at-all ones in the circle on the right. Everything else filled the middle circle. This is what I like to call our 'interest graph', the stuff we want to learn about with varying levels of seriousness, focus and consistency. It doesn't make any part or thing lesser, but merely gives it a different set of rules.

The focus ones demand a lot of depth, consistency and seriousness.

The fun ones are sporadic and fleeting.

Everything else encapsulates the general things we want to know about, but don't feel the need to be experts at.

It's almost like a balance we set for ourselves when we need to choose between any two things. A way to prioritize one over the other. And if at times the choice is flipped in terms of prioritization because our gut and mind tell us to, then we can move these items to a different circle in the graph.

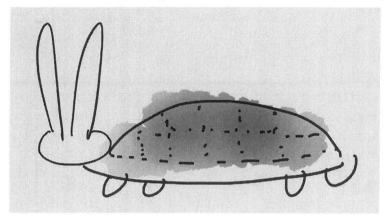

A Rabtle

All of us are rabbits and turtles in our minds. We have the ability to be both. It's just that the hybrid 'Rab-tle' inside us is a unique percentile mix for each of us. It's like calling all of us generalists and specialists when we're neither—we're hybrids. The world around us enables this way of being.

The more we realize that we have found something we truly love doing, the more we'll automatically do it. Dig deeper into it for a long time to come. And while we're doing that, we'll still be drifting through other interests. The dabbling and digging deeper will continue in this pattern till we start finding our interest levels in a particular thing overtaking what we'd been focusing on till then. This leads to that very thing we dabbled in becoming our primary area of focus.

Exposure to the modern world has made us better adapted for complexity, and that has manifested as flexibility,

with profound implications for the breadth of our
intellectual world.
David Epstein, Range: Why Generalists Triumph
in a Specialized World

The modern world, driven by the Internet, allows all of us to dabble in a multitude of things. It also allows us to constantly evolve our minds in ways that previous generations didn't have the opportunity to. That's what brings about terms like 'side hustle' and 'pet project'. The definition I personally like the most is 'multi-hyphenate'. It's a term I learnt while reading Emma Gannon's fabulous book *The Multi-Hyphen Method*. It's a way to list down all the things that we do as individuals and simply add hyphens between them. Put in the one you focus on the most on the far left, and keep adding more next to it towards the right as you move from the serious interests to stuff you dabble in but feel focused enough to add under your name.

Dispersing yourself and straddling multiple interests
will make you better at each one because you are constantly
improving and being challenged in multiple ways.
Emma Gannon, The Multi-Hyphen Method

We drift from focus to focus, but that doesn't mean we can't focus. It just means we can't focus on only one thing. It's the variety that keeps us going. There is no 'one size fits all', and no 'one focus fits all'. It's just the pursuit of finding things that interest us and holding onto them till they do truly interest us.

The Present Holds the Key to the Way Ahead

Pay attention to what's in front of you—the principle, the task, or what's being portrayed.

Marcus Aurelius

The future seems hopeful and exciting, the past feels like lost time that demands reminiscing and nostalgia, while the present seems ordinary and mundane. This feels especially relevant looking back at the last two years of our lives, doesn't it? Nostalgia is at its peak, and there is a constant sense of dismay about our present. But it isn't just about the last two years. There is so much more to it.

We often avoid what we have to do right now by telling ourselves we're focused on planning for the future. We hold off on our to-do list for the day because we've come across a podcast talking about the 'future of ____' (fill this with anything that we would read or listen to just to avoid work). And as the time thinking about the future eats into the time we need to work on the present, we let our to-do lists get overloaded and run behind schedule, we turn to our phones to de-stress, and before you know it, the future has arrived and it feels unremarkable, like a lost opportunity. So, we tell ourselves we need to be positive and not bury our face in a cushion and lie in bed all day in a stream of 'meh' and woe. But that just makes us feel worse. And this spiral goes on till we find a way to turn it on its head.

20

Imagine an alternative scenario. You spend your day working on the present and your evenings and nights focused on the future. You slot time for yourself, you optimize time for work and you allow yourself to feel the way you are feeling (seriously, go ahead and mope on that couch; I do that often enough myself). Sounds good? Well, this isn't an ideal scenario—it's actually something you can embrace by making some simple changes to how you deal with your daily focus, your future mapping and your inner feeling.

Let's start with the daily focus stuff.

> A man can stand anything, except a succession of
> ordinary days.
> Johann Wolfgang von Goethe

Most of us know what we need to do every day—which task is the main focus for that day, which is a priority and what can be scheduled for later. But we pick the easy one first, thinking we'll start off slow. I've subscribed to the 'let's do the tough stuff later' school of thought for ages. My standard reason was, 'I need to warm up first', and I would always follow that up with 'I do my best work at night'. So, the productive part of the day would start too late, and by the time I hit my stride, it would be late at night, and I would often be left struggling to not let today's task spill over into tomorrow till I realized it was 2 a.m. But that being said, let's be honest. None of us want to sleep early and wake up early. It feels like an 'old person' thing to do. No one said burn the early morning oil; there's a reason why the phrase is 'burn the midnight oil'. So, nights were my chosen time to get stuff done. And then 'ego depletion' as a concept came into my life and made me question a lot of things.

Ego depletion is a psychological concept that likens our mind, especially the prefrontal cortex, i.e., the part that focuses on self-control and willpower, to a battery with a limited daily charge. When we wake up in the morning after getting adequate sleep and rest (adequate sleep being the key point here), our willpower battery is fully charged. That's because when we sleep, this specific part of our brain is dormant. It's also why, as we get deeper into sleep, we dream. So, when we wake up, we find ourselves with the mental strength to focus, and that's why if we begin our main task first thing in the morning, it gets done quickly.

> *Early to bed, early to rise, made Johnny healthy,*
> *wealthy and wise.*
> *Unknown (although I suspect my*
> *kindergarten teacher)*

You'll often hear of CEOs and entrepreneurs waking up before the world wakes up to get their work done. It's because when your mind is primed to perform and you don't have distractions around, you bring your A-game. I wrote a third of this book waking up at 6 a.m., churning out words and ideas before everyone else at home woke up.

What we also see is that as the day goes on, this battery of willpower depletes. We slowly lose the energy to focus and withstand the temptations of the world around us (including our phones). We don't just feel our energy dwindle, but we also often find that we need to push ourselves harder to get the ideas and breakthroughs we seek.

But that doesn't mean this is the only way. Not all of us have to become 'morning people' or give up on our nights. The key aspect is to get enough sleep and rest. We must understand how our system flows from peak performance all the way down to needing rest and rejuvenation. We need to find those elements that can help us figure out how to build an approach that's adoptable but still inherently built for us.

That was for the long term. In the short term, if we can't get enough sleep at night, we need to ensure there are enough breaks during the day. Take small gaps or micro periods of 'switching off' when we aren't looking at our phones; when we can close our eyes and tune the world out; when we meditate or zone out or just go for a walk, even if it's just around the room—basically anything that doesn't require us to focus deeply or control our mind. I equate this to charging our phone's battery during the day so we have enough charge to last the day.

Another thing I will urge you to do is establish winding-down and waking-up rituals for your day. Stay away from your devices for the last half an hour before you sleep, and stay away from the same devices for the first half an hour after you wake up. Let your mind cool down and warm up like you would during a workout. Get the big task done first, and then let the madness begin. The day won't seem as stressful any more.

In reality, most of us can adapt and change how our day is organized over time to optimize for our needs. I was listening to Quentin Tarantino on the Joe Rogan podcast the other day, and he talked about how he switched from being someone who would write all night in a bar and wake up late every morning, to someone who got his writing done in the afternoon, lazed in his pool in the evening and went out for dinner at night (seems perfect, doesn't it?). Tarantino said he did this to tune his clock to the world and yet function with focus when he had to.

So, if Quentin can, why can't you?

Let's now look at the future and understand one simple fact. *We have no idea how the future will turn out.* So, we shouldn't prepare a plan for the future; rather, we should double down on today in a way that we're better equipped for whatever the future might bring.

It's important to think about what you can do today that will give you better odds tomorrow. Wisdom, health and wealth, in that order, give you better leverage that anything else. Tim Ferris, in his book *Tools of Titans* refers to 'health, wealth and wisdom' as forming the tripod our lives are balanced upon. If you have a vague idea about what trends might scale in the future and have the energy to build towards them and a robust foundation to hold you steady, then your odds of failure are as minimized as possible (although they're never negated; the last two years are a case study in why you can't predict the future). Future proofing yourself, your career and your business requires two things above all else: focusing on the present and accepting whatever the future brings with a smile.

> *Don't seek for everything to happen as you wish it would, but rather wish that everything happens as it actually will—then your life will flow well.*
>
> Epictetus

Not everything we wish for will come true. Nature and logic always have other plans. And because we make plans for the future in our heads while ignoring the present and tell ourselves these plans will come to fruition, the blow is harder when they don't. We then proceed to curse fate and the world for conspiring to ensure our failure. Over time, we come to accept our fate, but we lose both time and energy in the cursing phase.

Stoic philosophy speaks of something called 'Amor Fati' or 'a love of fate'. It says that since all we have control over is the present, we must focus on the now and accept our fate with open arms. It tells us to not waste time on broken dreams but look at every failed dream or plan as fuel to do better, to progress further. Use this failure to channel greatness, or just plain progress, into ourselves. Anger is easy, acceptance is hard. Focus on the present so we can build the trust in ourselves to better embrace the future. Lauren Martin in her deeply moving book *The Book of Moods* speaks of this:

> *I trusted myself to live in the present, in a way that would take care of my future self. And the more I trusted myself, the less I saw myself worrying about the future.*

Living in the present is tough. It requires us to face not only our life as it is but also our feelings as they truly are. And more often than not, we don't feel great or motivated or happy. Life can suck very badly at most times in the present. So we try our best to ignore how much it sucks by finding distractions anywhere we can. We scroll through feeds of happy images and looped videos of fun, we doom scroll through randomness and binge watch to disconnect. And we often emerge feeling like the world seems happier, more productive, motivated, shinier and basically more fun than our present. We then resolve to turn our frown upside down and be positive. But, before you say, 'What if I don't feel like being positive right now', wait!

Understanding and embracing how we feel at any given moment, and being true to our feelings and what we have in front of us, can give us more clarity and focus than any fake sign of positivity. Mari Andrew in her book *My Inner Sky* speaks of choosing 'present thinking' over positive thinking. She said that to stay resilient, she needed to embrace how she was feeling in the moment, rather than embrace a positivity that wasn't in her vision set.

'Present thinking brought beauty and goodness into my life, whereas positive thinking just made me feel like I was choosing the wrong emotional state,' Andrew wrote.

Positive Thinking Doesn't Equal Happiness

To be able to find renewal within ourselves to bounce back and move ahead, we have to be honest with ourselves and explore our emotions. Because the one thing that clouds our mind the most is unresolved feelings and emotions. And the best way to move ahead is to face them and listen to them, not sweep them under the rug.

So, embrace how you feel at this present moment and allow yourself to feel and heal as genuinely as you can. The lack of this is why we keep turning to nostalgia or future gazing—we don't want to face our present. But the world changes in an instant, and so can the space you occupy in it. All you need to do is keep an eye on where your feet stand and your heart lies.

Questions Aren't a Starting Point, They're Markers for the Road Ahead

Research and homework are vital, but deep knowledge comes from doing, from getting your hands dirty and from asking the questions others are too afraid or embarrassed to ask.
Ronnie Screwvala, Dream with Your Eyes Open: An Entrepreneurial Journey

How many times have we stopped ourselves from asking a question, clarifying a doubt or just digging a little deeper into something that sparked our curiosity? All because the voice in our head holds us back by saying:

'What if my question makes me sound ignorant, or worse, stupid?'

'Maybe I should try figuring it out myself, why ask?'

'People don't like too many questions, it irritates them.'

'I'm sure it isn't that tough, someone would have asked a question otherwise.'

It's that constant voice in our head telling us that we shouldn't speak up for fear of being labelled stupid, irritating or worse, uncool. But questions aren't a means to an end; they kick-start many beginnings. They help us learn, understand and expand our minds like no other action can.

I was the kid who would always have a question, who would want to know how things worked and how they were made. I was truly a curious cat for everything seemingly useful and definitely useless.

But it's uncool to ask too many questions! So, somewhere along the way, 'coolness' became more important than 'understanding'. And the questions dried up. But then I learnt a trick that helped me bring the curious cat back from the uncool zone to the 'you're in charge' spot.

Now I can't for the life of me remember the source of this trick (I'm also generally averse to claiming I came up with something), but it's been one of the most effective tools in my arsenal. It's served me well in different ways at different times in my life and career. At most times, when I have a question in a professional setting, I start with, 'I have a stupid question.'

That one word, 'stupid', works like magic. Here's why.

A: You're setting a low bar for yourself by calling the question stupid, so the pressure on you feels lesser.

B: The people around you also don't judge you too much because, well, you've already said it could be stupid.

C: If it turns out to be not stupid, then you're a lot cooler than if you hadn't stated it was stupid in the first place!

It's like how our brains are wired to not complain about something being too hot or too spicy if it has a label that says, 'This is very hot and super spicy'.

It's the same for the disclaimer about mutual funds too. 'Mutual funds are subject to market risks, please read the offer document carefully before investing.' The disclaimer is read super-fast at the end of every mutual fund advertisement, but what it's driving into your head is, 'Something can go wrong with this, so be careful with it.'

There is also another interesting quality to using the word 'stupid' before you ask a question or even put across an idea. This is specifically for when you rise up the ranks in your profession, become a little senior, as they say, and take on leadership positions. Let's admit it: no one wants to call out their boss for saying something that doesn't make any sense. So, if you're the boss or lead and you want to get value from the crowd around you (as you should) and not just hear the sound of your own voice (as you shouldn't), then using the word stupid can give great results.

This is how I use it.

I start any question or idea I have with 'I have a stupid idea'. It's almost like a free pass to anyone in the room to call out or state their perspective on my idea. Most people I've worked with for a while know this is a tool I use, but they play along because they know I'm doing it to give them a free pass.

But questions don't just end there; they're also navigators in a journey of learning from others. Over the last few years of hosting over a hundred and fifty podcasts, I've realized how much a good question can teach not just the person asking but even the person responding. Here are a few of my observations and guidelines.

The quality of your questions determines the quality of your life.

Tony Robbins

A question is always better than a statement. Because a statement that ends with a question mark invites the other person to contribute, to add their two cents, to truly get involved in the conversation.

It also takes away any perceived imbalance in stature or hierarchy between the conversing parties. You need to be on a level playing field to have a conversation, otherwise you're just two people shouting from different floors of a building and that's definitely not enjoyable for either of you. Always remember that it's not about prodding or playing a game of one-upmanship. Rather, it's a way of finding something deeper and more evolved than what was stated in the first place by keeping the door open to various points of view.

The core value of questions often lies in the art of true listening. Let's face it: we all spend more time thinking of what we want to say than we do listening to what's being said. When we truly listen and base our questions on what the other person has said, we do two things.

Firstly, we show that we're listening, that we're interested. And that helps the other person respond and vibe better with you. It shows you care about what they're saying, and so they start caring about what you're about to say.

Secondly, when we listen to others, we notice navigational strands from what they've said. It could be a line, a word or an inferred thought. And those strands lead to great questions and responses to take things ahead. They help navigate the conversation well.

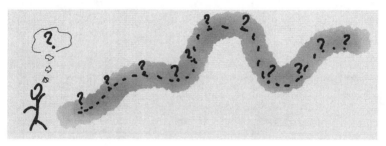

Questions Can Lead the Way

Let's look at an example. 'I don't get how people don't like pineapple on pizza. I mean, it's the perfect blend of all the flavours of a pizza with this amazing addition of sweetish saltiness!'

Now this can lead to any number of questions.

'I wonder how the whole pineapple on pizza thing started. Do you know?'

'Is there a way to package the pineapple pizza experience differently so people aren't averse to it?'

'You mentioned the blend of flavours, and it's actually a great point to dig into. What do you think the balance of those flavours is?'

While this is an endless debate (FYI, I'm on the 'I like pineapple on pizza' team), I hope you understand what I mean about finding a question inside a statement.

It's like you're on a treasure hunt and there are clues all around that you're trying to find to lend structure to your way forward.

Questions are something I would equate to life itself. We spend our lives asking questions and using the answers to find our way, and at some point at the end of the road, when we look back, we'll ask ourselves, 'Why don't people like pineapple on pizza?'

An Actual Poll I Ran on Instagram with over 120 Votes

CHOOSE

'IT IS OUR CHOICES THAT
SHOW WHAT WE TRULY ARE,
FAR MORE THAN OUR ABILITIES.'

Albus Dumbledore

Luck Gets You through the Door, But It Doesn't Ensure You Stay

In my experience there is no such thing as luck, my young friend—only highly favourable adjustments of multiple factors to incline events in one's favour.

Obi-Wan Kenobi

In 2005, I hit rock bottom in life.

I was living a dead-end life in a one-room apartment in Bengaluru. I was still struggling to finish my engineering degree (which I should have ideally completed the year before) and was spending my nights working for AOL's cancellations division (they called it the retention department). My job was to make sure every customer who called to cancel stayed a customer. I would clock in at 2 a.m. and take calls till 9 a.m. Needless to say, my sleep cycle, general health and head space weren't in the best shape.

But I was out of options. I had in many ways resigned myself to this stalemate my life had found itself in. I had failed to wrap up all the modules with the bare minimum grades in my engineering degree. I had tried to hide this from my parents until I had no option but to tell them. I had planned to go study in the US, get an MBA and live the American dream, but everything was on hold till I could actually complete the remaining modules and get my college degree. The job at AOL was my desperate attempt to not go back home a failure, to have a reason to stay back in Bengaluru, to not face the reality of my life. Or rather, to not face the fact that to make something of myself, I'd have to take some tough decisions that required asking myself some serious questions. But I wasn't ready.

It was around that time that my mom mailed me the application for a media school that I could apply to. It was her attempt to give me a lifeboat as I drifted aimlessly through life, to wake me from the stasis I had set myself into. Ever since I can remember, I'd wanted to work in the media industry. I practically spent my teens on a couch obsessing over MTV (as you read in the last chapter). But that wasn't the only reason why I gravitated towards the application. It appealed to one of my quintessential traits. My mom had given me something that has always been a fundamental part of me throughout my life: *a possible alternative.*

It was a reason to quit what I was doing and go looking for something else. I've done a lot of quitting so far in life, from picking and dropping different sports, ever-changing career choices, giving up on relationships and fluctuating ambitions. Once you give me an alternative, I always moved towards it, dropping whatever I'm doing at that moment.

This is something many of us do and the reason for it is simple. Quitting is easier than sticking with it; pushing through difficult or even mildly tough situations demands internal fortitude from all of us and we find it simpler to give up. Now I'm not saying you shouldn't give up; rather, you should give up when your rational mind tells you that the better option (not the easier option) is to give up.

Another reason we give up is because we give our mind too many options. Then we either drown in indecisiveness for too long, or worse, get confused about what it is that we really want, what our true self wants.

Matthew McConaughey put this beautifully in his book *Greenlights*. 'Too many options can make a tyrant out of any of us, so we should get rid of the excess in our lives that keep us from being more of ourselves. When we decrease the options that don't feed us, we eventually, almost accidentally, have more options in front of us that do. Knowing who we are is hard. Eliminate who we're not first, and we'll find ourselves where we need to be.'

Once we eliminate who we're not, it's easier to figure out who we are. So, instead of conveniently hiding behind a multitude of choices, wiping out a bunch of them gives us fewer options, leading to lesser procrastination and a whole lot more clarity. But I wasn't there as a person yet.

So, I quit my job, went back home and proceeded to lie on the couch in our living room. The very concept of preparing for the entrance test of the media school was a fleeting thought that appeared from time to time, but my mind wanted to switch off. It refused to face the fact that I'd have to put in the work. I was non-committal, lazy and zoned out.

And soon enough it was time to take the test. As I reached Bengaluru the day before the test, I had two choices:

1. Get a haircut and meet a friend for a drink, or
2. Study and get a good night's sleep.

I chose the first. So, there I was, entering the exam hall the next day, slightly hung-over and quite unprepared. And it was at that point that I decided to take an instinctive gamble on what I was going to do.

The test was for multiple schools within the university I was applying to and the media school was just one of them. Each school within the university had a specific weightage they assigned to each section of the test. So I made a calculated guess that for the media school, the only two sections of the entire test that could be relevant were English and general knowledge. I answered those two sections, ignored the rest and walked out.

I never looked back. I went back into my state of stasis, looking for another job like my last one so I could tune out the world. And then one day around noon, I was woken up by a call from an old acquaintance. 'Congratulations on making it to the next round on the test, man!' he said.

I just turned over and went back to sleep. There was no way I had gotten in. He was definitely mistaken. But then curiosity and FOMO got the better of me. I checked the website and sure enough, there it was—my name on the list of people called in for the next round of the admission process. Until then, I'd never gotten in through merit into anything in my life, having relied on my parents to find me a way in. But now, through a calculated gamble and some luck, I'd actually got a foot in the door.

This story can be a case study of luck giving someone an opportunity they didn't truly or fully work for. And I would agree with you. I hadn't taken the test seriously and had gambled with a chance I had been given to find the light at the end of the tunnel that was my life. And the gamble had paid off. But what's more important about this story isn't about my luck paying off, but rather the choice I needed to make afterwards.

Because let's face it, life does throw us a bone from time to time. Opportunities fall into our lap, chance encounters open up doors, and at that juncture, we can choose to do one of two things.

We can feel lucky and continue the way we've been operating, which means we can hope that luck gets us through the next round as well. Or we can look at it as an opportunity life has given us and shake ourselves out of our stasis.

For the first time in my life, I chose the latter. As I sat down that night, it finally sank in that I had an opportunity to actually do something in life, something I had in many ways always wanted to do. If I didn't follow up this instance of luck with a different mindset and actions and truly leverage this for my own good, then this spark would burn out as quickly as it had shown up, and I'd be back to being lost in the fog of choice stasis.

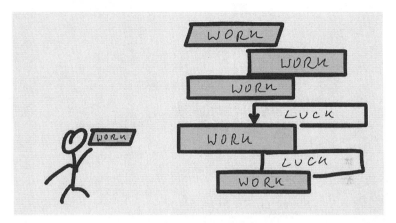

Luck and Work Are a Game of Jenga

We know that life is splattered with a little luck for all of us. What we often discount is the importance of our actions after luck has kicked in. In my case, I did focus a little more on the choices I made after that entrance test, and it became the start to the next chapter of my life, one that helped me find my spot in the universe. When an appetizer of luck is followed by a main course of pure personal effort, we get to enjoy the dessert of success. The alternative is to constantly look at menu options all our lives.

Always take a chance on better, even if it seems threatening.

Ed Catmull

The Gaps in the Wall Help You Scale the Wall

Life sends you down funny paths. And you get many opportunities to keep your eyes open.

George Lucas

'Hey guys! This is Varun, he's the designated village bicycle. Anyone can ride him!'

That was on my first day as an intern at MTV.

Now I know what you're thinking. That's not a kosher thing to say to someone on day one of their internship! However, back in 2006, this was pretty much par for the course, and while it was meant as a joke, most of us hadn't realized we should do better. Leaving that aside, MTV in 2006 was the best possible place to be an intern at, or just be around, period! The best way to describe the vibe in the office would be to imagine every form of awesome content on YouTube and Instagram being created in one place, with all those people, all those set-ups, all that madness in one place. That was MTV during that period.

I had always dreamt of working at MTV. It was practically my education system in the early 90s, spanning music, pop culture, what was cool and just about 'what was everything'. And there I was actually working (or rather interning) at the one place that had shaped such a large part of my mind. I had four months to soak in whatever I could of this place and hopefully figure out a way to actually get a job there.

Now, let's pause for a second and think about life as an intern. You get into an organization thinking you're going to do so much; you'll live and breathe and create what you've been dreaming of. But in reality, most of the time you're relegated to doing the grunt work (the stuff no one wants to do), or worse, the bare minimum, which means you'll be in and out of the organization without having added any value to you or anyone else. These things happen because, to the people working in the organization, an intern is merely a temporary extra hand who can help, someone who will soon leave and so there's little point in over-investing in training them. So before you blame the people interns report to, it's important to look at it from their perspective as well. But there is a win-win scenario for both employees and interns. I'll get to that in a bit.

I started off with the grunt work, which in those days was logging tapes. (For those from a different time: all television content used to be shot and stored on magnetic tapes, unlike memory cards today.) My job was to note down time codes on a ton of tapes along with the piece of music that was used in a particular show. Detailing what time during the show it was used and for how long (that's how artists who made that music got paid).

It was a lot of monotonous work. And after two weeks of this, I decided a change in strategy was needed if I wanted to get anything meaningful out of my internship. Without an actual plan, I ended up using what was in hindsight a three-step strategy that changed the trajectory of the rest of my internship and became something I still use to this very day.

In between logging tapes, I popped into every shoot, every edit, every brainstorming session, open conversation and even occasionally a smoke break group (I quit smoking twelve years ago and it's one of the best things I've done for my health and life, but back then, I used to smoke!). And unless I was shooed away—which happened sometimes—I stuck around happily in the background with my ears and eyes wide open. Most of the time, we feel the need to add something to every scenario we're a part of, but often all we need to do is listen. (Please refer to the previous chapter again for context.)

That was Step 1: Pay attention and understand the machine.

And slowly, I saw how things worked, who did what, who worked with whom and who was more open to ideas than others. This scoping exercise is of paramount importance for anyone looking to blend into a new company or system. If you don't understand the beast, it'll never be your BFF.

Then there was Step 2: The right time to speak is as important as what you say.

'What do you know about this again?'

I was in a brainstorming session, and the man who headed MTV shows at that time was Raghu Ram, the guy who arguably blew up the Indian reality TV scene. On that day, he was leading a brainstorming session on a new show MTV was planning. Generally, from what I'd observed, when Raghu Ram asked for a point of view, most people below a certain position in the pecking order stayed silent.

'Don't talk unnecessarily, he doesn't like it.'

'Don't try to be cool, he doesn't appreciate it.'

'Keep your head down and do the work. Only speak up if you're a hundred per cent sure.'

That was pretty much the range of advice I had got earlier from the other 'juniors' who were slightly senior to me. But that day, when he asked a particular question, I raised my hand and said, 'I have a thought about this.'

That's when he said, 'What do you know about this again?'

'Not much,' I replied, 'but I've watched and read about a lot of this stuff. So I still feel like my thought can help.'

The room froze, and everyone was looking at me like I was a dead man.

Raghu paused for a few seconds. Then he smiled, sat down and said, 'Tell me more.'

And soon I was assisting as many producers as I could on their shows, sitting in on edits and even acting in any possible role on camera. But I didn't automatically get those opportunities. While I listened (Step 1), I also kept a mental note of the gaps in everyone's needs, the stuff they didn't want to do, didn't have the time to do or have anyone to hand off to. Everyone had one or two extra things on their plate, or something they were struggling with, or worse, an irritating thing they would rather not do. That's where I came in. By listening and engaging, I found the gaps in the wall, and all I had to do was offer to fill them in.

You see, the more you keep your eyes open, the more opportunities you spot. Many people call this 'being proactive', but I beg to differ. I'd say this is being 'strategically active', because you aren't saying yes to everything. You're saying yes to the things you want to do that are need-gaps for someone else. Needless to say, I didn't log tapes for the rest of my internship, and four months later, I left deeply satisfied and a whole lot richer in experience.

And that's Step 3: Do the work, no compromises.

Once you find the gaps and fill them in, you have to do the work. Don't compromise, just get it done and do it well. I slept in bunk beds we had in the office on many nights instead of tiring myself out in transit. I took showers in the office on occasion (we thankfully had a shower). On most days, you would spot me walking around the office in my boxers with a cup of coffee during the wee hours of the morning. That was until one of the producers told me, 'You don't have to live here to do a good job. Find some balance now or you never will.' I listened to that advice and ensured that I still went out, had a life and found some semblance of balance.

I did the work. When you're an intern or just starting off, you must put in 200% effort. You must also ensure that your effort is seen and, more importantly, remembered. We're often told that we need to keep our head down and do the work. I'd say you also have to look up and let people know you did it. Only then, when you leave and people feel the void you leave behind, will they remember that it was you who filled it.

This holds true for any job, but it's doubly true for any internship. That's why I always like to call every internship a sliver of opportunity. We can learn not just what we can do and how to do it, but we can also make other people want us to work with them. We can move past what seems difficult to find what appears to be an opportunity. That's when we can wedge that door open and make the place and the work ours.

Wedge Your Way Ahead

One: Out of clutter, find simplicity,
Two: From discord, find harmony,
Three: In the middle of difficulty lies opportunity
Albert Einstein

We need to follow this in life as well. Move towards opportunity by scanning the scenario, learning from the people who are already in it and doing the work. Just these three seemingly simple steps will let you take informed choices of action. Otherwise, you're leaving it all to luck, which doesn't hold true or fast in the long term.

It's Not about the Journey or the Destination

There are a series of popular quotes you get if you google 'journey, destination quotes'. They all go something like this.

'The journey is the destination.'

'Success is a journey, not a destination.'

'Happiness is a journey, not a destination.'

And my personal favourite greeting card quote: 'It's about the journey, not the destination.'

As amazing and thoughtful as all of these sound, let's be honest. They're all kind of one-dimensional. Think about it: if all that matters is the journey, then you're never reaching an end point that truly satisfies you! Or to put it simply, if the end result is smaller than the process of getting there, it would bum you out, wouldn't it?

Now, I am in no way dissing this concept. I'm a total propagator of satisfying journeys, but I think we need to look at this whole 'journey-destination' story a little differently. Let me start with a story about two guys I once met on a train who had the most amazing journey I've ever heard (and I'm pretty sure ever will).

It was the year 2000 and I was eighteen. I was barely into the fourth hour of a twenty-four-hour train journey back home from boarding school. I was travelling on the cheapest tickets I could buy, which was all I could afford (I confess, I'd spent the money my parents sent me on an all-night binge with my friends). So there I was, lying on my berth at midnight, bored and hot. I was also bummed out, having realized that I had packed just two cigarettes, one of which I'd already smoked.

Just then two European guys boarded the train, and within a few minutes, they opened up a fresh packet of cigarettes and started smoking away. I was pretty sure I'd ask them for one sooner rather than later, and was planning my 'Hey, can I bum one?' strategy. Then I noticed that they were trying to buy water at every station where the train stopped, only to find that pretty much all the stores had shut for the night. So I swooped in and offered them my bottle of water, and casually bummed a smoke in return. As we smoked, I asked them how their journey was going, and what unfolded was the weirdest story I'd ever heard.

The guys—let's call them X and Y—were from a small town in Switzerland. They had worked small jobs for the last two to three years to save up for the travel they had planned. Their first stop had been Mumbai, then two months in Goa (cliché, I know), and from there, they had switched two trains to mine on their way to Chennai. So far, it sounded like two typical backpackers, until they told me what they were planning to do next. From Chennai, they would go to Puducherry to learn how to surf for two months, and then fly to Thailand, where they would learn Thai boxing for four months. After that, they planned to go to Australia and work odd jobs for six months to replenish some of the money they would have ended up spending backpacking and diving off the coast, before finally flying to Brazil. There, X would head back to Switzerland, sell everything the two of them had and then fly back to Brazil to join Y and proceed to set up—wait for it—an Internet cafe.

For an eighteen-year-old, that was the most underwhelming end to a very interesting journey that I could think of. I still remember looking at them dumbfoundedly. After all that journey, their idea of a showstopper was setting up a place where people would come to surf the Internet! But they seemed perfectly happy with the idea of ending up where they intended to. And while I continued to chat with them through the night, I felt both confused and underwhelmed by the ending.

I have no idea what happened to X and Y. Maybe they didn't ultimately set up that cafe. Maybe they decided they just wanted to go back to Switzerland. Or maybe, one day I'll walk past a banner advertising the 'World famous Thai boxing champions from Switzerland'. Now that would be a good ending!

This story keeps coming back to me when I think about where I'd like to end up in life. And it gives me three perspectives that I think everyone needs to consider.

Firstly, if our short-term goal or destination isn't properly defined at a given point in time, then our journey is just a state of random motion. Even our search for experiences is often led by an innate raison d'être (reason for existence). There is an innate reason for our motion. I was once asking a friend, fellow entrepreneur and podcaster and pastry chef extraordinaire Pooja Dhingra, about her focus on trying new things. She told me that she gives herself one goal beyond her career every year. For one year, it was to run the marathon; for another, it was to learn French so that she could deliver a keynote speech in French in Paris in front of hundreds of people. These yearly experiences she signs herself up for have had a profound and enriching impact on her life. And this impact goes far beyond the realm of the experiences themselves into every aspect of her life.

Secondly, having a small, even underwhelming eventual goal might take us through more interesting stops along the way. It'll make us value the right kind of experiences in the short term, and yet ensure that we pick what is important, relevant and exciting in the moment rather than a compromise. Or as Joseph Campbell put it, 'If you do follow your bliss, you put yourself on a kind of track that has been there all the while waiting for you, and the life you ought to be living is the one you are living . . . follow your bliss and don't be afraid, and doors will open where you didn't know they were going to be.'

Thirdly, we shouldn't take ourselves or our lives too seriously. Rather, we should look at them through the right lens of authenticity, which in turn breeds humility. Because when we don't build mountains in our heads, we enjoy learning how to climb walls a little bit more and maybe even master the art of the climb better.

> *Our potential is one thing. What we do with it is quite another.*
> *Angela Duckworth, Grit: The Power of Passion and Perseverance*

I've often in my life been called the guy 'who has so much more potential, if only____'

I was someone who could be creative if he wanted to, could be great at academics or sports or business or . . . (the list is a little long, so I'll let you fill in anything you want. I'm pretty sure it will cover something I've been told I had the potential to be better at if I had only worked towards it.)

For many years, as I hopped from one interest to another, one career opportunity to another, I developed a lack of confidence of ever achieving whatever my supposed potential was. It also resulted in my trying a bizarrely varied set of things in work and life. In many ways, all of it has added up to bring me where I am today.

If I hadn't tried and failed at many a sport, I wouldn't have found my love for a hybrid form of daily fitness. If I hadn't worked (or tried to work) in everything from being a whisky promoter in a bar, a reality TV producer, a wannabe actor to even a call centre executive, I wouldn't have the toolkit of skills that I've used through my journey as an entrepreneur, podcaster and more importantly, a human being.

We are the sum total of our experiences, and if we reduce the pressure of the ultimate goal, then we will eventually figure things out.

This doesn't just apply to how you approach your path in life, but also to how you see your path as it connects to others. It's what I often think about when I consider my role as a father to our daughter Leia. Being a parent doesn't mean having razor-sharp, defined goals for my daughter and me as one entity, neither is it a journey that can be mapped out like an exact synchronized science. It is a fluid process of gauging every day, every choice, every moment in a way that isn't just built on logic but a foundation of pure love that has no parallel. She can be a resounding pain in the butt, and yet, she is so much more than anything my heart has ever felt. She is her own person as she should be.

> One of the best things you can do as a parent is to realize that your child is nothing like you, and everything like you.
> Jenny Lawson, Furiously Happy

My daughter's journey is her own, but is a core part of mine too. I am here to help her make choices in life, but her journey and her destination are her own. I am here to be there for her, yet let her be; to be both parent and silly friend; to hold and to hug; to advise and guide her for her own well-being, but allow the choice to be her own; to feel her arm on me when she sleeps and yet, be open to that arm wanting some independence as she grows up. That is the essence of the choices we face in the journey of our lives. She is my life, but her life is more than me, and I just need to play my role through every moment in the best possible way that I can. My place in her overall journey or her eventual destination is not important; rather, it's my choices in the moments where I am needed that truly count. It's not about me, just the part of me that is there for her and the whole of her that is in my heart.

So, it's not about what's bigger or more important between the journey and the destination, but how they balance each other in the overall scheme of things and what they achieve in every moment. Stuff happens to us while we're on the journey of our lives, it makes us instantly shift goalposts that we had previously set in stone. That's the whole point of journeys and destinations—every step of the journey gives us a new destination.

Make Yourself Multidimensional by Looking Inwards

Let me ask you two questions.

What did you love doing as a kid that you don't get enough time to do now?

What are the things you've enjoyed doing as a grown-up that you keep wishing you had more time to do?

Write as many answers as you can think of to both the above questions. Then, pick only those that you would do not for money, but just for the love of it. And from these, choose a maximum of four things.

Put them all in one square. Let's call it Square A.

Next, list down all the things you do in your career. Not just what you say you do, but drill them down into the stuff you actually end up doing, like making presentations, pitching ideas to clients, building creative ideas, working with data, managing or being a part of a team, etc. From this list, pick four that you believe will be crucial for your career to grow the way you want it to.

This is what we'll call Square B.

Now hold on to both of these till the end of the chapter. First, let's think of ourselves as kids for a moment.

I've always believed that we have three animals within us since we're kids: our career animal, our creator animal and our soul animal.

Square A and B

We're all born with the creator animal. It feeds our curiosity, our sense of imagination, our flair for doing the stupidest and yet most fun-filled things. When I think back on my childhood, I recollect spending hours playing with toys and action figures and coming up with full-fledged stories of drama, action and adventure. The tiled roof of the house I grew up in was a mountain I needed to scale to rescue a princess (side note: princesses don't need rescuing; in fact, quite often, they're the ones who actually save the day). I used to be the dancer, the entertainer, the one who had an immense amount of useless information to constantly share.

Then, when we get to school, the career animal comes along, telling us to focus on the 'serious', 'future-building' part of life. It can't all be fun and games! There's education, grades, career, adulting and stuff that always seems to have 'mature' as a prefix.

'It's time to take the mature decision.'

'Think with maturity.'

'Life's not all fun and games, you need to grow up and be mature.'

You know the drift.

Slowly but surely, the career animal takes over and the creator one goes into the 'hobbies' section of the farm in our mind. Meanwhile, the soul animal silently sits as the balance between these two opposing beasts, holding our character in its grasp, evolving along with the dynamic between the career and creator animals.

Some people are lucky enough to combine their career animal and their creator animal into one hybrid beast at an early age. But for most people in a predigital era, this would mean a dynamic where the career animal ruled the roost, and defined the essence of the soul animal and therefore our character. This isn't to say that the career animal couldn't be fun, but rather that by letting one side rule, we ended up being more one-dimensional as we grew up.

There will be moments when you have to be a grown-up.
Those moments are tricks. Do not fall for them.
                    Jenny Lawson, Furiously Happy

Today's world has turned this concept on its head. You can have a day job and a career, and yet be a creator and artist too. The Internet has allowed the creator animal to come out of the woodwork and become an equal player in shaping our character. And in emerging from the 'hobbies' section, it has enabled the multi-hyphenated individuals that I mentioned earlier. It has also busted the myth that careers need to be serious and everything else is just fun and of no value.

By allowing multiple dimensions of ourselves to emerge, grow and bloom, we aren't just feeding our interests. We're using them to fill in the gaps in our own repertoire of skills. This makes us far more interesting, engaging and often more fun and knowledgeable to be around in a multidimensional way.

I've seen this transformation first-hand in my journey as a creator. I went from this outgoing, entertaining, nonsensical 'yappity-yapper' as a kid to a teenager and young adult who found safety from his own insecurity by blending into the background. I took what the world threw at me—both as personal failures and societal norms of adult behaviour—as a sign that I needed to be the silent, mature guy. The one who took responsibility and who behaved and acted like it. The guy who would briefly unleash the kid inside him from time to time but who largely stuck to the grown-up role.

Then podcasting came into my life, and by unleashing my creator animal, the kid was back. Slowly but surely, he returned and brought balance. I still held on to the positives of my adulting journey, but I brought back and unleashed the side of me that liked creating, that enjoyed being a freewheeling conversationalist (that's a better term than 'yappity-yapper', I guess). And over the last three years, this changing dynamic has done much more than merely help me find happiness in a space I had long forgotten I enjoyed.

In allowing this balance to grow, I've been able to make my professional side at The Glitch, as well as my investor side with a few start-ups I advise, a lot more interesting and multidimensional. I bring the randomness of my creative side some structural balance through my experiences on the professional front. Both sides win, so I win!

By allowing my career and creator animals to coexist in an equal dynamic, my soul animal has bloomed more than ever.

You can work this out yourself, even if you haven't figured out your creator focus. There is a way to build dimensions to yourself that you might not even realize lie within you.

Let's go back to the two squares.

Put them next to each other and take some time to evaluate how each element in one square can help in the other square. Think back on the time when, as a kid, you would connect the dots or match things that seemed like they had connections. Do exactly that now.

It takes some time to get the hang of this part, so don't rush. Mull over it, go back to your original lists and revise the four in each square if you need. Eliminate things that in hindsight don't ring true for you (refer to the chapter on luck). For instance, when you ask yourself what you like, you often add a lot of things both because you feel you should like them and because you aspire to like them. So, to get this exercise right, you must learn to scratch off things from the list as much as you have to connect the dots.

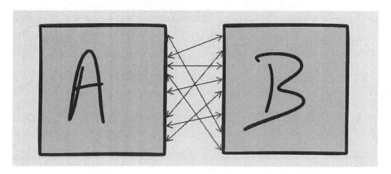

Connect the Squares

Elimination is such a simple yet straightforward way of figuring out who we are. I've often struggled to put a label on who I am, and this method has helped me peel away what I know I'm not. Because the less complex you make this process, the clearer your path becomes to conjoining your animals.

And eventually, you'll discover patterns of how one side can help the other flourish. See what will take less effort to kick-start and which parts in your profession these can actually benefit from. This isn't meant to be a perfect science, but rather a way for you to list out the dots that lie hidden in your mind and find ways to connect them.

As Austin Kleon puts it in his book *Keep Going*, 'Creativity is about connections, and connections are not made by siloing everything off into its own space. New ideas are formed by interesting juxtapositions, and interesting juxtapositions happen when things are out of place.'

LEARN

'KNOWLEDGE IS KNOWING
THAT TOMATO IS A FRUIT. WISDOM IS
NOT PUTTING IT IN A FRUIT SALAD.'

Miles Kingston

Learning Is So Much More than Education

We spend a quarter of our life in pursuit of formal education, from school to university and then progressively upskilling ourselves for the sake of career and other such grown-up prospects. While we pick up a lot of knowledge along the way, most of us fail to soak in enough wisdom.

Knowledge is abundant. Deriving the right insights from knowledge and using them at the right time in the right way is wisdom. Because let's face it: most traditional forms of education suck. The very structure on which the system of traditional education is built is based on the need to create an industrialized supply chain of like-minded individuals by feeding them the same information in exactly the same way and through the same medium. Of course, there are amazing examples of education being done right even within traditional means, but I attribute them more to the teachers evolving the process rather than to the system itself. What traditional education mostly doesn't take into account is that we as human beings are different from each other. We are different in the way we learn, the way we absorb knowledge and even more in the way we distil that knowledge into our version of wisdom.

Take the way we learn, for instance. The human mind can absorb information through multiple forms. Some might prefer a visual form of learning, while for others, audio might be the best way to get the content into the mind. We might prefer reading it from a book or article, or we might need to feel and experience the topic at hand in a physical form for us to truly absorb it. This system of differentiating the ways in which we can learn through the medium that facilitates the learning is called VARK, short for visual, auditory, reading/writing and kinaesthetic. While none of us is a hundred per cent focused on one medium, we all have varying percentages of the mix that works best for us to learn. Audio might help us absorb certain kinds of information better, while visuals can help us remember specific points more clearly, and the experience of feeling an object can teach us more about it than any textbook can. Our learning ratios may differ, and how each of us consumes content on the Internet is proof of that. We learn more and more on a daily basis by watching content on YouTube or listening to a podcast or reading a book or just getting our hands dirty and trying stuff out. We learn in different ways, and a 'one-size-fits-all' approach will never work if we want to optimize the infusion of knowledge into our minds.

> Knowledge is something you possess. Wisdom is something you do. It is a skill and like all skills, one you can learn. But it requires effort. Expecting to acquire wisdom by luck is like expecting to learn to play the violin by luck.
> Eric Weiner, The Socrates Express

In the road towards lifelong learning, we often spend too much time dumping information into our minds and little time reflecting on it. We don't put in enough effort to truly soak in the insights and nuances and find newer angles to what we consume. In the sea of abundant knowledge, wisdom sometimes has no space to swim. And I have to be honest: for the longest time, I would consume as much content and information as I could just so I could talk about it with someone else or bring it up in a brainstorming session or use it in a social media post. In my endless search for things to feed the flow, I didn't take enough time to truly learn from the information I was spouting. And there is an innate danger to going down that path, as it leads to arrogance and insecurity.

Arrogance is ignorance plus conviction. While humility is a permeable filter that absorbs life experience and converts it into knowledge and wisdom, arrogance is a rubber shield that life experience simply bounces off.

Tim Urban

How often have you been in a conversation with someone who keeps spewing random facts to give themselves an opportunity to speak, but then never goes beyond the surface? That same individual when questioned takes it personally. That's what surface-level learning does—it gives us a thin skin and a fragile ego, because deep down we know that we don't know anything beyond what we've read. What many of us do is what many schools taught us, which is to 'mug up' or 'by-heart' or just remember by rote. This too is because we haven't built a system around learning, one that focuses on knowledge distillation, diversification and subtraction.

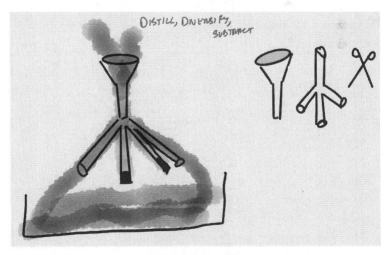

Distil, Diversify, Subtract

One clear system I've built recently for knowledge distillation is a system of cataloguing and storage. We can't remember everything we read, watch or listen to. Over time, our mind will push unused information out. But that doesn't mean you can't catalogue it. Keep notebooks, keep a folder on your computer, start a note on Scribble, the note-taking app, and always add things to it. You can choose to meticulously catalogue it or, like me, scatter it across a multitude of physical and digital storage units and rummage through all of them when you want to go back to something. Although it's supremely disorganized, the rummage method has a great bonus value to it: while you're looking for something else, you end up coming across a lot more stuff you've stowed away. So it's like unintentional revision every so often. And the more you go back to something, the more embedded it is in your mind and the deeper you understand its core.

If you do want to go deeper into this concept, the 'Three Whys' method is a good place to start. This was something I came across in Chip Heath and Dan Heath's book *Made to Stick: Why Some Ideas Survive and Others Die*. The method is simple. When you're trying to understand the emotional core of a particular thing or idea, write down why you think people are doing it, and then write down why it is important three times. You'll notice that each successive answer takes you deeper into understanding the true nature and core of the idea as well as the emotion behind it.

Then comes the question, 'How do I diversify my knowledge base?'

In Austin Kleon's books, I came across a concept called 'content family tree'. Let's say you have an individual you follow for the perspective and knowledge they impart to you through what they create and share. If you take note of who they reference, what they read, watch, listen to or just connect with in a systematic way, then you have more knowledge to consume on what you already relate to. This often helps you dig deeper and gives you a more diverse perspective, especially when you check out people the individual doesn't agree with as much but references often. It's almost like the way Netflix throws more content on to your home screen based on what you browse, watch and engage with.

As with monetary investments, this investment in knowledge providers and their connected sources also requires your focus to be long term, deep and diversified. In other words, build a diversified information portfolio.

> *Progress requires unlearning. Becoming the best version of yourself requires you to continuously edit your beliefs, and to upgrade and expand your identity.*
> James Clear, Atomic Habits

I've been in the content business since 2006. My job was to help execute everything from television properties of all scales and sizes to brand commercials, live shows and beyond. I've been through almost all parts of the process, from assisting across departments, to directing, producing, writing, editing and, if the project was unlucky enough, camerawork as well. I've enjoyed working on various formats of content, and so I've always prided myself on having a macro perspective in the content space. Or at least I did till I became a creator.

Once I started learning about how people create content today, how they break many established rules and processes that have been followed for years—stuff that was considered fundamental to the storytelling and story-creation process—I realized that I didn't have to learn new things as much as I needed to unlearn a ton more. In fact, as I kept unlearning since putting on my creator hat, I've also realized the many things I've done wrong over the years. I let myself get comfortable on the 'knowledge cushion'. I rued the multitude of times over the years when I said, 'This is how it's done!' or 'Why break what doesn't need fixing?' or just 'I've done this before, let me explain!'. Although conforming to past knowledge is often intended to speed things up and get things done, they often become roadblocks to rethinking the wheel before the road evolves. That's why unlearning needs to be a constant process in our learning cycle. We need to constantly question established thoughts and use them more as reference points rather than the endgame.

So, spend every day learning, distilling, diversifying and subtracting from your knowledge pool. Spend time reflecting on your day and understand what you've learnt from it. Use all the knowledge you've collected to guide you in finding clarity and wisdom from your own life.

That's what wisdom is at the end of the day—our mind finding clarity and driving us forward through our actions, reactions, perceptions and reflections.

Don't Just Follow Tradition, Learn From It, Question It and Evolve It

In Russian folklore there is an archetype called yurodivy,
or the 'Holy Fool'. The Holy Fool is a social misfit—eccentric,
off-putting, sometimes even crazy—who nonetheless has
access to the truth. Nonetheless is actually the wrong word.
The Holy Fool is a truth-teller because he is an outcast.
Those who are not part of existing social hierarchies are
free to blurt out inconvenient truths or question things
the rest of us take for granted.
Malcolm Gladwell, Talking to Strangers

During the early days of the COVID-19 lockdown, I developed a morning ritual that has taken on a whole new meaning for me.

It involves a moka pot.

A moka pot is a classic, old-school, Italian coffee pot that helps you make 'espresso-like' coffee on a regular stove. The process is simple, and it doesn't really demand anything fancy.

You fill hot water into the bottom compartment of the pot, place the coffee filter above it and add the coffee powder on top (this demands a finer grind than most). Then you screw the top compartment on, place the whole thing on a stove and wait for

An Amateur's Rendition of a Moka Pot

the coffee to flow out. It works off a pressurized system which is pure genius. As the water boils, it flows upwards from the bottom of the pot, through the coffee in the filter before dripping through the central spout of the top compartment into the holding area (the drawing above helps explain this better). The reason why it has the thick consistency of espresso is because the coffee flows up from the bottom under a certain amount of pressure, which makes it richer in texture and density.

It's the only way I like my morning coffee now. I even bought myself a smaller one that I carry on every trip out of town, and everyone who accompanies me rolls their eyes at it. It got the same reaction from my poor mother too, when she saw me pull it out to make my coffee when I visited her.

But do you know, I actually bought that Moka pot on my trip to Italy for my honeymoon eight years ago! It was one of those classic, old-school things that I loved, but once I came back, I stuffed it inside a cabinet and went back to my regular coffee machine. Using the pot felt like too much effort.

Somehow, in the middle of a global lockdown, I created the ritual for myself. It was born out of a need to feel some old-world normalcy that was based on using an age-old traditional coffee pot to brew my coffee every morning. It's a feeling of nostalgia that hits home every time.

So, when someone tells you that tradition and nostalgia can't bring simple joys and happiness into your life, tell them to try using the tools tradition provides.

This is just stage one. You can either stay here and be stuck in nostalgia (which is often a great place to be in), or you can let it become the launch pad or foundation to something bigger. Don't just stick to the moka pot, go beyond it. Nostalgia can fade if you keep repeating it, but using it to spark your curiosity can be the start of a whole new journey.

That's what I did. I began to research different ways to brew coffee, old and new, different roasts, even temperatures (if you haven't tried a cold brew, you must). And as I went down this rabbit hole, I also found different ways to use every single tool that can be used to make coffee (some old and some new). Then came stuff that goes with coffee, the accompaniments that make a cup of coffee taste even better. I started identifying the subtle flavours, the variations in aroma and the purity of the experience of drinking coffee. Over time, it's become a core part of my daily routine (although I don't drink coffee after 4 p.m. to ensure I sleep well at night).

If I'd just stuck to the moka pot and not done anything else, my joy would have in all probability been momentary, but now it's a constant stream.

This is something all of us can apply to every aspect of our work and life. To discover the new we need the old, because everything that is new has been built on the foundation of something that has come before. All the knowledge of the past and all the information from the present can help us visualize and create the future. So never scoff at tradition—learn from it, absorb as much as you can about it. But, and this is the most important condition, don't think twice before questioning it and reshaping it as you see fit.

In his phenomenal book *Ride of a Lifetime*, Robert Iger says, 'I know why companies fail to innovate. It's tradition. Tradition generates so much friction, every step of the way.'

Tradition isn't sacrosanct. It should not demand blind faith, and it's not something that cannot evolve. Tradition is what history and experience teaches us so we can make informed decisions. It's like creating content for social media or a blog based on actual data.

Everything needs a starting point and tradition gives you that. But if you want to move ahead, you have to leave the starting point behind and evolve from it. So while you must internalize the tradition and understand it, you must also analyse how it should be evolved and transformed for the needs of the now, in today's context. Don't let it hold you back and only dwell on changing something simply because others believe it needs to be done a certain way. See how you can evolve from it in a way that adds true value to you and all the others.

Most of the time, we get stuck between two groups, people who have faith in something and those who want to question every aspect of it. The right idea for the times lies somewhere in between, and it can only come from understanding both ends and building on it.

A Pain in the Neck Can Take You Down the Right Rabbit Hole

Let's start this chapter with an exercise.

Sit up straight and look directly in front of you.

Slowly turn your head to the left till your chin is parallel to your shoulder blade.

Hold for ten seconds, then raise your chin towards the sky and hold again for ten seconds.

Lower your chin and return your head to your first position.

Now turn your head towards your right till your chin is parallel to your shoulder blade.

Hold for ten seconds, then raise your chin towards the sky and hold again for ten seconds.

Lower your chin and return your head to the first position.

Tilt your head towards your left shoulder blade without turning your head and hold for ten seconds.

Tilt your head towards your right shoulder blade without turning your head and hold for ten seconds.

Come back to the first position.

Look down till your chin rests on your neck and hold for ten seconds.

From this position, look up as far as you can without turning your head and hold for ten seconds.

Come back to the first position.

How does your neck feel? You're welcome.

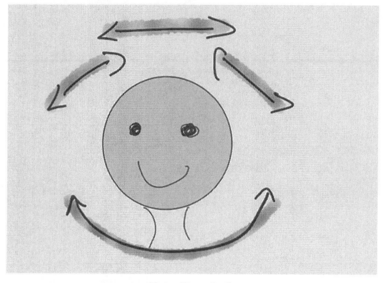

Twist, Turn, Smile

Have you ever had a pain so bad that it took over your life? I have. It's a pain in the neck, literally, and it's a huge part of my life. I would even go as far as to call it the single largest obsession in my life.

On most days, I wake up with a feeling of soreness, stiffness and a seething pain every so often in the area around my neck. For some time, I ignored it, put it down to the after-effects of my training in the gym and the way I sleep as the probable culprits, and waited for it to subside. But the more regular it became, the more I started to obsess over it. A few years ago, I was out of town to attend a conference and woke up one morning to a searing pain in my neck. I was walking around in pain all day till someone handed me a tube of muscle pain-relaxing cream (thank you, kind soul). As it brought relief, I started looking up creams and cold therapy oils, and after multiple searches an article on stretches popped up and my life changed forever.

Over the next few years I read articles, watched YouTube videos, subscribed to Instagram accounts and found any and every resource I could on the kinds of stretches that would relieve soreness. I found a treasure trove of chiropractors who turned stretching tutorials into musical reels on Instagram (@dr.remix_), and strength coaches who focused on techniques to not just train correctly but also recover and eliminate pain (@thereadystate). I discovered yoga moves, biomechanics, functional strength training methods and decompression breath techniques. I even read about how different kinds of pillows and sleep positions could help me. I still obsess over stretching techniques that don't just help my neck but also relieve any other niggle or soreness. I went down a deep rabbit hole and it made me all the richer.

Now, why am I telling you this?

All of us have everything from minor niggles to major problems in our lives that trouble us and continue to haunt us. We tend to ignore them or curse them, but actually do nothing about them. I say we must obsess over them. Problems stay problems till we decide to find a way to solve them, and the solution often lies in starting with admitting that we have a problem in the first place. We must identify and address the elephant in the room and obsess over solving it. And the first step is to ask the right questions and start learning as much as you can from the answers.

Try to absorb as much knowledge as you can about the problem at hand. Learn, ask, search for any and all information around it. The more we learn, the less of a niggle it will be; it will transform from a problem to a gateway of learning. This also helps fight the biggest impediment to knowledge and learning—ignorance! Or rather, our tendency to be satisfied with our own ignorance. All the months I spent saying, 'I guess it's because I worked out wrongly,' or 'Maybe it's the way I sleep,' or 'It's just something people with a long neck have to live with,' were months I spent ignoring the fact that I didn't know enough to come to a conclusion and lacked the mental drive to fight that ignorance.

Ignorance can be a tricky pitch. It solidifies our sense of 'knowing enough' and teaches us to ignore basics of learning like evidence, logic and time-tested techniques. Tom Nichols in his book *The Death of Expertise* puts it beautifully, 'Not only do increasing numbers of laypeople lack basic knowledge, they reject fundamental rules of evidence and refuse to learn how to make a logical argument. In doing so, they risk throwing away centuries of accumulated knowledge and undermining the practices and habits that allow us to develop new knowledge.'

Swimming in the sea of our own ignorance is one of the fundamental issues most of us living on the social web have. And what's worse than ignorance is the semi-ignorant amateur, someone who has read one article or watched one video and believes they are an expert through a false sense of confidence. This false confidence suppresses the humility that ignorance often brings, and makes us overconfident, arrogant and self-centred. We learn something to make ourselves seem smarter than we are and not to actually make ourselves smarter than we were (read that twice and it hits harder). It is this fear of seeming ignorant that fuels our sense of arrogance. The Sorcerer supreme explains this to Doctor Stephen Strange in the Marvel movie *Doctor Strange* when she says, 'Arrogance and fear still keep you from learning the simplest and most significant lesson of all. That it's not about you.'

The only way to beat this is to understand that we need to constantly keep learning, and not limit ourselves to just one aspect and perspective of our learning. We should try to become thought leaders, or rather, thought drivers or navigators—people who learn everything they can about a subject before talking about it. And we should help others use whatever we've learnt to enable their own journeys. That is the singular focus that drives me as a content creator, right from my first day as a podcaster to now hosting multiple podcasts and creating YouTube/Instagram content, writing a newsletter and even working on this book. All these creative channels have been driven by my need to satisfy my curiosity about things I don't know, all of which end up being stuck in my head, like an itch that needs scratching. And all I try to do is ask, read, listen and learn to not just bridge the gaps in my knowledge due to my own ignorance, but to find rabbit holes that I can keep going down.

That's the key—to constantly be in learning mode and never claim to be an expert.

This drive will keep you going down that rabbit hole and help you not just accumulate knowledge but also truly find wisdom. We need more rabbit holes in our lives to keep us rolling down the road to knowledge. So, find your pain in the neck and start from there.

Failure Is the Best Teacher If You Actually Pay Attention

'Next contestant, Varun Duggirala.'

I was twelve, in my balloon pants and shiny shirt, the kind MC Hammer made popular in the 90s and which then Prabhu Deva extended into my young pre-teen mindset.

Breakdancing Essentials: MC Hammer Pants and MJ Glove

Those pants puffed up as I moved, which in my head screamed 'cool'! My trusty leather glove was jammed onto one hand (you can't not pull some inspiration from Michael Jackson after all). Now, this was peak summer in costal Andhra Pradesh, which meant on a cool day, the temperature was around forty degrees. Needless to say, the backstage area at the 'Lions Club of Kakinada Break Dancing Contest' was a sea of sweat with blobs of balloon pants and leather gloves and a few glitter-and-satin shirts thrown in.

I'd been preparing for this all month. In the previous two years of trying to be a competitive breakdancer, I'd failed to make it into the top three. But dancing was always my happy place (it still is on many days), and I assumed I had the ability to win the contest. But I didn't!

So, every year, I added more pizazz to my look, and spent a ton of time finding the right music track and adding new dance moves to it. This year, I was going to jump off a small stool onto the stage and move into a classic Michael Jackson step. I'd made a mix tape that blended three songs into each other with crucial moves at each point. My pants had glitter on them that year. Confident and pumped, I jumped onto the stage, and didn't make the top three again. I was told I had stood fourth, but in hindsight, every kid's parents must have told them that.

I was shattered. I felt like a failure. I never competed in breakdancing again.

I have danced in many a crowd since then (my general range is the classic 'Bollywood uncle' moves but with enough flexibility to avoid getting the 'uncle' tag), but I've never tried breakdancing again. As I went deeper into the learnings I gleaned from my failures, this story came back to me, and I soon realized why.

But before I get into it, here's the customary clichéd quote on failure. 'If at first you don't succeed, try and try again.'

Here's another. 'Try, try, never say die.'

How many times have you had clichéd lines like these thrown at you when you face a roadblock or any form of failure? The glorification of failure is an oft-used motivational tool. The very concept of a failure helping someone progress rather than stalling the pursuit of their life goals is part of every entrepreneur hack guide or hustle porn manual. It's not that I don't agree with this perspective. But my innate issue with the way failure is glorified is that most of these glorifications don't capture a particular nuance that you need to add to the essence of 'failure as a tool'.

So let me clarify again: failure is an amazing teacher. It has taught me a lot in my life, and I know I've failed more than I've succeeded at most things I thought I'd be good at. Case in point being the breakdancing contest, as well as most aspects of school and college, broken relationships, my many attempts at being an actor or director or even a writer, and finally the innumerable failures during my journey as an entrepreneur. When I look back at all these failures, I realize that the things I eventually found success at had the additional nuance to them.

The nuance is what I like to call 'iterative improvement'. The point of failure isn't to try the same thing all over again. It's to learn from it and do a tiny bit better in the weaker areas, change direction slightly or go about it with a completely fresh outlook when and if you try again.

The point of being iterative is to understand what was fundamentally wrong with what you did in the previous iteration and correct the core issue the next time around rather than succumb to superficial changes. It's like spraining your ankle in a race and deciding to change your shoes rather than question your technique and training. It's easy to make such superficial changes and try again. What's tougher is going to the heart of the problem and being honest with yourself about why you failed, what you really need to change and whether it's even worth trying again.

Let's go back to the breakdancing story. My idea of improving was to add a couple of things: more flair and drama (superficial improvement), and new moves and music (because adding new things makes old stuff better).

But what I didn't change or work on was that my moonwalking sucked and so did my 'hands on glass' move. These were literally the main acts of my performance every year and I couldn't do them (I honestly still can't). That's why no matter how hard I tried to cover up the fact that my ability to do 'the fundamental steps' of breakdancing was weak, it was there for everyone to see.

So, at the end of the day I'd always lose. If I had reflected on this honestly at the time, I could have sidestepped the fundamental flaw by either learning the steps or just avoiding them (you can do an entire sequence without either of the steps), but my inability to be true to myself resulted in my failing consistently. I hadn't learnt from my failure.

> *Stepping in shit is inevitable, so let's either see it as good luck, or figure out how to do it less often.*
> *Matthew McConaughey, Greenlights*

This simple aspect applies to everything we fail at in life—we never sit down and address what actually makes us fail. We never honestly tell ourselves that we're often doing the most obvious thing wrongly. The reasons why we fail can be both minuscule and glaringly obvious, but in either case, if we don't look in the mirror, we can't see what's wrong. Only when we are absolutely honest with ourselves can we learn from our failures. And if we don't introspect and address them head-on, these failures can very easily become a crutch on which our future failures can be blamed.

I've sucked at being organized and focused all my life, and I've admitted this publicly. I blamed it on a self-diagnosis of ADHD or attention deficit hyperactivity disorder, and used this as an excuse for many a failure, both professional and personal, resulting in failed relationships and professional crises. It's an easy crutch to fall back on.

Only when I finally went to meet a certified therapist to understand how my mind worked did I come to the root of the problem. It wasn't that I lacked the ability to be structured. I just suffer from a personality that strives for autonomy. I have an innate need to chart my own path. If I'm given a goal and asked to get to it my way, I will succeed, but tell me the exact steps to get there and ask me to follow them to the T and I will fail. This realization has fundamentally changed how I operate in life. It's made me build systems from scratch (mixing multiple references most of the time) in most things I do, and I can say that I'm ten per cent more organized than I was last year (which is nothing but iterative improvement).

It's like Al Pacino said in his fabulous half-time speech in one of my favourite sports movies of all time *Any Given Sunday*, 'You only learn when you start losin' stuff. You find out life's this game of inches, so is football. Because in either game—life or football—the margin for error is so small. I mean, one half a step too late or too early and you don't quite make it. One half second too slow, too fast and you don't quite catch it. The inches we need are everywhere around us. They're in every break of the game, every minute, every second.'

So, if you fail, don't just try again without adding that small piece of learning into the mix, that small step of improving or that extra moment of reflection. Otherwise, you'll just end up with a teacher in failure whom you never seem to learn from.

If at first you don't succeed, learn and evolve from it, and then try again!

Boredom and Inspiration Go Hand in Hand

I don't dream at night, I dream at day, I dream all day; I'm dreaming for a living.
Steven Spielberg

I want you to do a small experiment with me. It's something I make my four-year-old daughter do from time to time.

Lie down on your bed and stare at the ceiling. Look at the fan go round and round, let your eyes wander over the entire ceiling, observe every nook and corner. Don't reach for your phone, don't have a conversation with anyone, don't try to find something to do beyond focusing on the ceiling. Slowly a feeling will creep in, one we all know but seldom allow to persist these days. It's called boredom. Stick with it, let your mind wander if it wants to. As time passes, you'll start thinking of stuff you haven't had time to focus on, stuff that's been gestating as seeds of ideas in the corners of your mind, even things you've saved for a rainy day that lie covered in the avalanche of information your mind consumes—all of it will suddenly come under the spotlight.

There is a common joke that the best ideas appear when we're in the shower or in the loo. Often, the ideas come to us just as we're falling asleep or in the middle of the night in our dreams. What we don't realize is that when we're in the middle of an activity that puts

Let Boredom Fan Your Inspiration

our mind on autopilot with no fresh rethinking needed (when our RAM/'Random access memory' is getting some much-needed rest), suddenly we give our mind enough space to think, to come up with ideas and thoughts that don't crop up when we actually sit down to ideate or create. That's because the prefrontal cortex, the part of our brain that enables us to stay focused, relaxes when we're doing tasks that don't require much thought to execute. The mundane nature of these tasks reduces the need to concentrate and enables our mind to wander and look at things beyond what we're doing, and in many ways, we derive inspiration and ideas when we're in this state. That's why a lot of writers and artists take to alcohol and other intoxicants; the relaxing of the prefrontal cortex brings ideas to light. (As I learnt in Edward Slingerland's fascinating book *Drunk*, the correct amount of blood alcohol at which our ability to take big creative strides gets accentuated is 0.08 per cent or two small drinks). But overdoing this way of inducing creative spikes isn't healthy or even long-lasting. Plus, when the blur is excessive, you won't remember the ideas you have. So, while it's great to romanticize this kind of lifestyle, it can be severely damaging on many counts.

Boredom induced by mundaneness or repetitive tasks is almost like sparks that induce creativity. It allows us to trick our minds into feeling like we're in a form of stasis that has freed us from having to focus. Interestingly, it even happens when we're ill and on medication and lying in bed. There is a fabulous story about how James Cameron came up with the idea for the movie *The Terminator*. While he was filming *Piranha II*, Cameron fell very ill. So ill, in fact, that he was delirious and having weird, vivid dreams. One such dream was him being chased through a power plant by a cybernetic organism that kept telling him that he's been targeted for termination. The chase was dramatic, with Cameron trying to get away and the machine getting closer and closer, until he woke up in a cold sweat and wrote the idea down. And that's what became the story of the movie and the Terminator series. Sounds almost surreal, right? But then, think about your own dreams.

How many times have your dreams or daydreams been vivid enough for you to feel like they're real, or that the solution to a problem you have been struggling with for days comes to you just as you zone out, go for a shower or allow yourself a good night's sleep?

Sleep is an interesting example. Matthew Walker, one of the world's foremost experts in sleep science, has a counter to the popular hustle culture slogan 'I'll sleep when I'm dead'. He says that if we don't sleep well, we will definitely die early. He also provides a great perspective on the potential of tapping into optimal REM sleep (rapid eye movement sleep is when we hit our peak deep sleep, our eyes start to move randomly under our eyelids and we start to dream). He says that optimal REM sleep allows us to tap into the true power of our minds and our subconscious to solve all that we are trying to solve while we're awake. If you want to experience it yourself, try waking up after a good night's sleep and working on a big problem you've been trying to crack, and you'll find that often the solution comes to you a lot easier. This is also why a lot of people speak of the virtues of solving our biggest tasks at the start of the day. Overworking our mind, not allowing it to rest (and dream) doesn't drive us towards solutions and learning, but rather drives us away from them.

Avoiding work is the way to focus my mind.
                                Maira Kalman

But our ways of avoiding work aren't helping us in recent years. What do we do when we want to take a break? We pick up our phones, which are anything but relaxing for our minds. We live in a world of instant gratification though constant distraction, and this volume of distraction keeps our minds engaged and our dopamine levels high at all times. And what is dopamine?

Dopamine is a chemical found naturally in the human body. It is a neurotransmitter, meaning that it sends signals from the body to the brain. Dopamine plays a part in controlling the movements a person makes, as well as their emotional responses. It plays a role in how we feel pleasure.

The more dopamine we release, the more pleasure we feel, driving us to find more ways to release it. The Internet, especially a lot of modern social platforms, induces a constant stream of dopamine release in our minds. It's like a rush we can't get enough of, and once we put it away, we get feelings of withdrawal and deep restlessness that gets the better of us quickly and forcefully. I say this because I too am guilty of giving in to this feeling, just like so many of us. Like many things in life, it requires moderation to stay on the right side of the line between satisfaction and addiction.

Try bringing to mind a place you generally find peaceful.
Then tune in to specific sensory details to deepen your
focus and create a calmer state of mind.
                Meredith Arthur, Get Out of My Head

Excessive and constant dopamine release doesn't allow us to get bored. So the need to put that phone away so we can actually give our mind time to space out is needed now more than ever.

In most cases, the solution is meditation—sitting down and focusing on our breathing for an extended period of time to help our mind reset and relax. Let's be honest, most of us struggle with meditation. I know I do. My mind has always been a busy street intersection where I jump from idea to idea and distraction to distraction like jumping over the roofs of cars in a traffic jam. When I tried to meditate, I didn't even last two minutes, let alone the hours people seem to be able to do it. So as I failed, I sat up, reached for my phone and googled 'How to meditate'. And that was it, down the rabbit hole I went again.

But if you too can't meditate for extended periods, all is not lost. It just might be that for people like you and me, our form of meditation or taking pauses might be to go take a shower, take an extended loo break, go for a walk, just sit and stare out of the window or maybe even wash the dishes (this last one is my personal favourite). Find ways to tune out the noise and unleash our mind. Find moments of stillness in your life. Lao Tzu famously said, 'The mind tends towards stillness, but is opposed by craving.'

So, find ways to not reach for that phone, or open that app, or switch on that show. Build into your day periods of disconnection, monotony and solitude. That doesn't mean you must become a monk meditating in the mountains. You can be a high-performance individual *because* of these moments, not in spite of them. You just need to find your way to achieve stillness or taking a pause.

Your form of taking a pause might be to just tune out the world, with your phone away from your hands, while you allow your mind to wander. To sit near the window and watch the world wake up in the morning, to draw or scribble or doodle, to write on a blank piece of paper, to listen to music (lo-fi and jazz as genres are my personal recommendations) or just lie down and stare at the fan and let your imagination fly.

Your mind needs that reboot to find the time to wander into your subconscious and fill your idea base with something new, solve something you've been struggling with, or just sow the seeds of inspiration and allow your mind to bloom again. Because if we don't have the space to let it grow, then all we will be left with is the noise that we already have and no space for something new to find its voice.

> Stillness is what aims the archer's arrow. It inspires new ideas. It sharpens perspective and illuminates connections. It slows the ball down so that we might hit it. It generates a vision, helps us resist the passions of the mob, makes space for gratitude and wonder. Stillness allows us to persevere. To succeed. It is the key that unlocks the insights of genius, and allows us regular folks to understand them.
> Ryan Holiday, *Stillness Is the Key*

Mentorship Isn't a One-Trick Pony

The Worst Kind of DM

Hi!
Seventy per cent of the cold DMs people send on
social media

We all seek mentorship. It's a basic human trait to look to someone for advice, knowledge and just plain perspective. To turn to those who have achieved, learnt and have a deep understanding of the things we seek to grow in. But in a world filled with self-appointed thought leaders, 'growth hackers' and supposed motivational gurus, the search for a mentor and the desire to become one start with the same word: 'why'.

It's crucial to understand why we need a mentor. If we go after every bright, shiny object we come across, turn to them for advice and follow that advice exactly as they say it, there is a fair chance it will all go sideways. That's where the 'why' comes in. We need to have a clear reason for turning to someone, and this reason defines not just who you turn to but also what kind of relationship you need to build with them.

Is it to learn or imbibe specific knowledge?

Is it to get a point of view on where you are in your life and career?

Is it to include them in your journey as a guiding light in a clear and specific way?

Is it to leverage their equity and knowledge to further your career and business?

These four points broadly cover most mentor–mentee relationships. In my experience, the way to tap into each of them is as follows.

Is it to learn or imbibe specific knowledge? *Consume the content they put out, read their books, learn from their words.*

Is it to get a point of view on where you are in your life and career? *Attend a workshop, course, masterclass or live AMA (ask me anything) session they conduct.*

Is it to include them in your journey as a guiding light in a clear and specific way?

Try to get an exclusive slot with them to answer specific questions! In most cases this can be a direct message or email, although there is a large chance they might not respond.

Is it to leverage their equity and knowledge to further your career and business?

Don't just ask them for things, show them the value you can provide as well. Give equity, provide a service for free, surprise them with an offer that would make them smile more at your audacity and thought than anything else.

The clearer you are about what you need and what you can give, the better this will turn out. You often times start off your mentor–

mentee relationship on point one and over time move towards points two, three and four. I remember how I met one of my mentors Roshan Abbas, a man who might be one of the gold standards of a multi-hyphenate. A master storyteller, he has done everything from hosting numerous shows across television, radio and the stage, built, scaled and sold companies, been a film-maker, podcaster and investor, and above all else, he is one of the best people to have in your corner.

I first met him when he came to our college to conduct a one-day workshop. Unlike most workshops, his was dynamic. It changed and evolved as it progressed. He started off by giving us a brief for a television show we had to come up with, but then he built on the brief as things like channel mandates, brand sponsorships, target audience changes, etc. came along. This is pretty routine for anyone who's even spent a day in the media sector, but he hyper-accelerated that process and made us go through in minutes what would take days in the real world.

Roshan didn't preach; he showed us how things were and gauged how we reacted to it.

Years later, we did an animation project for his company Encompass, and he happened to see it and asked to meet the guys who did the work. And later, when we met, he remembered us. Not just who we were but the idea we had presented.

'Good mentors don't just speak, they listen.'

A few months later, he asked us for an urgent favour for a movie he had just finished (the title sequence needed an overhaul and he didn't have the time and money to get it done). We did the work for no money and his mentorship in return. It was the best barter we ever did.

'They give true value and receive in kind.'

Roshan became the first investor we got on board at The Glitch, and he continues to advise us across the things we do till date. But he has never told us what we must do, and instead has always shown us opportunities, shared experiences and opened doors.

'Good mentors help you find the direction to take but don't roll the dice for you.'

He gave me a piece of advice as I started to give advice to others as well (and I'm paraphrasing).

'Give advice for free, without expecting anything in return, with humbleness and maturity, and it will circle back to you,' he said.

We often expect things in return for what we do for others. It could be a connection, a favour or just some advice. But not everything is a transaction, and we shouldn't treat what we give people as one.

As Panos A. Panay and R. Michael Hendrix distil it down in their book *Two Beats Ahead*,

> The challenge for us as creative collaborators in any field is twofold: First, to be confident in our own skills so that other people can call on us to use them. Second, to be curious about the others so we can build amazing things together, with a shared vision and purpose.

That's the whole deal with mentorship, isn't it? You don't have to be a guru or messiah. You just need to listen well, collaborate not preach, give a clear perspective and share what you've learnt through your wins and fails. Help others connect the dots and never make it about yourself. Be authentic and don't expect anything in return. Most of the time, people just need to know that they're not wrong, more than figuring out if they're right.

> A mentor is someone who allows you to see hope inside yourself.
>
> Oprah Winfrey

CONNECT

'THE BEST IDEAS START AS CONVERSATIONS.'

Jonathan Ive

Good Conversations Breed Invaluable Learning

Conversations have always been the one thing I enjoy the most about the human experience. The way we see and build our relationship with the world and the people in it is brought together and made whole through conversations. And yet, conversations are the least appreciated form of learning. This is a travesty, because they complete the cycle of action, reaction, reflection and progression like no other form can.

In early 2020, I gave a TEDx talk on how we can have more meaningful conversations. As I was brainstorming on the talk, I remember looking back at all the conversations I've had throughout my life and the value I've gotten from them. That's when it struck me that while we do have a lot of conversations in our lives, if we're asked to categorize them into 'meaningful' and 'the rest', the meaningful stuff isn't as large a set as the rest.

And there is a reason for that. We suck at having good conversations. Period! We dread

- saying the wrong thing,
- not appearing interesting, or
- just not being able to talk enough.

Considering the percentage of our lives that we spend having conversations, it's bizarre that we aren't taught how to actually have a good one. And by good, I mean good for us and the people we engage with. So, to get better at having conversations, we have to go about it in three stages:

1. What we feel,
2. What we say and
3. What we hear

Let's start with what we feel.

I was a kid who wouldn't stop talking. I'd wake up and start and you couldn't shut me up till I fell asleep again. But that's also because as kids, we aren't worried about being judged by people around us till the world tells us we're being judged. And then the switch happens. I transformed from the kid who spoke to every single person he met, engaging them with random facts and details from my life, to someone who would slink away and not say much because he felt he'd be judged for what he wanted to say.

The fact is that from a certain point in life we worry we'll be judged. We often feel that what we have to say might not be what people want to hear, or worse, what people will disagree with. So we don't try and play it safe.

This goes beyond conversations and seeps into how we behave. We walk into a room and feel like we're being watched. Like the world has started to move in slow motion, and every eye is on us, every ear is listening to what we're about to say, just to pull it down and rip it apart. We're feeling the spotlight effect.

The spotlight effect is a term used by social psychologists to refer to the tendency to overestimate how much people notice us. In other words, we tend to think there is a spotlight on us at all times, highlighting all of our mistakes or flaws for all the world to see.

In most cases, this feeling is shaped by our personal biases towards ourselves, which get reflected in our mind as the way people perceive us and are further accelerated by our own experiences. We think we see in others our own feelings about ourselves and our inability to do and say the right things. It makes engaging with the world incredibly daunting for those of us who suffer from a lack of confidence in general. It also leads us to question the decisions we've taken in our life, and drives our sense of validation (something we suffer from a lot, thanks to social media).

I spent a large part of my adolescence feeling judged for how I dressed, talked and looked. I felt I was constantly under a microscope that was focused on everything about me. It was like finding myself suddenly naked and on the street, and trying to figure out a way back into my apartment while being surrounded by people watching.

How can we pull ourselves out of this self-inflicted sense of being judged before we get to those who are supposedly judging us? Well, let me tell you about a three-step process I've been following in recent times that has helped me tremendously.

First, learn to block out the noise around you. Imagine you're the only one in the room. Close your eyes for a few seconds (if you can, or just pretend you're thinking deeply about something), take a few deep breaths and focus solely on yourself. It's like switching on noise-cancelling headphones—when you block out the crowd, you feel less intimidated.

Next, learn to observe how people react to you. They're usually more focused on their own insecurities than your performance. See them as who they are in that moment and not who you think they are. You're all swimming in the same sea of validation and insecurity. You can pull them out of it if you first pull yourself out of it. Realize, digest and remember that fact.

Finally, always think about the worst-case scenario. Not every situation is so earth-shatteringly important that it will make or break you. And even if it does, what's the worst that can happen? When you map out the possible consequences, the process becomes less scary.

So, the next time you feel like you're in the spotlight, take a deep breath, look at the others around you and think about the worst that can happen. It might be the best way to ensure that the worst never does happen, because when we look beyond the spotlight, we find the answer to our problems.

> By definition, we're blind to what we can't see. When looking for answers, we're like the proverbial drunk who only looks for their keys in places where the light is shining. That's why philosophers study both the ground and the spotlight.
>
> David Perell

Now, let's look at what we say.

Our responses in most conversations are built on reactions that instantly crop up in our minds. These reactions are built on what we have fed our minds over time. The more knowledge we possess, the better and faster what we want to say comes to us. This hasn't much to do with education per se, but rather about deeply evaluating whatever we pick up in the course of the information we consume every day. What we often mistake as clutter is actually strands of unused information that need to be organized into a system of what we consume and what we store in our minds. It's like nutrition for the mind.

I am an information hoarder. If I had to make a list of my core competences, 'information hoarder' would be right up there with 'relentless conversationalist' and 'overenthusiastic bunny'. I love knowing stuff—serious stuff, weird stuff, stuff that has no connection to anything in my life. I love it because it feeds my innate curiosity and enhances the other core competences I mentioned above.

I also specialize in something many call useless information! It's called useless by a large section of the people around us because it doesn't really connect with any form of 'career enhancing', 'academic excellence driving' or 'grown up vibe generating' stuff. But let's be honest, most of that stuff is quite boring and not as much fun.

Knowing a lot of random things doesn't (in most cases) help in standard academic pursuits or even regular careers. It does, however, help us become truly interesting. The stuff we know beyond the usual forms that element of us which we call 'Personality'. The more interesting the mix, the more diverse and intriguing your personality is. This can help us in every possible scenario in life and work. Let me explain.

Think of the nursery rhyme 'Twinkle Twinkle Little Star'.

'Twinkle twinkle little star,
How I wonder what you are,
Up above the world so high,
Like a diamond in the sky.'

It's something you know by heart. It's embedded in your mind. But let's say you've spent a lot of time going down the rabbit hole with Neil deGrasse Tyson (arguably the most popular astrophysicist of our times) on YouTube. Then to you, that poem might become,

'Twinkle twinkle little star,
I guess you might be a dwarf star,
How I wonder what kind of a dwarf star you are,
Red, yellow, orange or blue, I mean you could be a white dwarf too.'

I can go on, but you get the point. All that is information that got added to half a rhyme because of a bunch of content I happened to spot online one day (and saved for a rainy day, like today as I write this). It instantly differentiates my words from what anyone else might say when asked about this nursery rhyme.

Now, I know that was a weird and extreme example. But when you think of how to fill the time in those gaps before meetings start, or when you're trying to make small talk with a bunch of people you don't know, or when you're on a date and she/he asks you 'so what else are you into?', you have something interesting and non-regular to say. Hence, 'personality'.

I spent a large part of my adolescence being the guy at the back of the group who was scared to contribute to any ongoing conversation. Then one day, I decided that I'd contribute whatever I found interesting and what others often found 'non-regular' or atypical. At worst, people would think I was weird. In the best case, they'd consider me interesting. I've always found that the line separating weird and interesting is in the eyes of the observer and the ears of the listener.

So, hoard information and allow your curiosity to find its way around the maze. When you find something interesting, figure out a way to store it for a rainy day. That's what people have been scribbling away in notebooks for years, and these days the tools to store information are aplenty. Content curating and archiving apps to store articles, highlight repositories for stuff you mark in books, Pinterest boards, saved posts on Instagram—the list is endless. I use all these, and often spend hours trying to find stuff I've saved.

But save all of it, and use every chance you have to share it. The more you share, the more the number of ideas that roam the world (on a side note: verify what you share before you do. Sharing stupid conspiracy theories and fake news is bad. Be a good and responsible sharer).

Our innate ability to let our minds find, store and project information to everyone around us is one of the things that makes us truly human. Otherwise, we'd just be a bunch of people sitting around discussing the weather.

Which brings me to sharing like a human. Don't drive a conversation simply by stating stuff for effect and leverage, or to one-up those you're speaking to—you'll only be feeding your own sense of false superiority. Talk to people like you would want to be talked to, like a human being who wants to share something of value. And if you don't have something of value to share, 'Be sincere, be brief, be seated.'

That line by Franklin D. Roosevelt is something I often go back to. Whenever I feel like overstating my point of view and stretching something longer than it needs to be, or when I find myself trying to give my voice more space not because it needs it but because my ego requires it, that line pulls my feet back down to the ground.

Brevity has more power than it is credited for. If you can state something in the crispest manner, then not only do you get the point across, but you also lend it clarity and weight. Brevity teaches you the core pillar of a conversation; it's a two-way street, so being brief means you won't block the way all by yourself.

And that brings me to how we listen.

Most of the time, we (and I'm often guilty of this as well) switch off when the other person starts to speak or moves the conversation towards something that doesn't really interest us any more. But if we truly push ourselves to listen, there is much to learn even in the most mundane of things. Plus, it helps us develop better relationships when the other person feels we are not just truly listening, but are also an 'involved listener'.

We all focus on what we say and how we respond, or just how clever or interesting we can appear to be in the process of being involved in a conversation. And while we've all heard the line 'listen to converse', we haven't understood it.

In his book *Think Again*, Adam Grant touches upon this in the best way possible. He says,

Listening well is more than a matter of talking less. It's a set of skills in asking and responding. It starts with

showing more interest in other people's interests rather than trying to judge their status or prove our own.

Only when we're genuinely listening, showing interest in what someone else is saying and opening our minds to their perspective are we genuinely conversing. Otherwise, we're just talking. To converse, we need to listen, absorb and respond without judgement.

It's also why the best conversations are the ones with perfect pauses between one person saying something and the other responding.

The other advantage of being an involved listener is that if you feel the conversation is headed towards a dead end or an uncomfortable space, you can then listen to segue. Segueing means moving from one topic to another seamlessly, without making it seem abrupt. It's an art form used masterfully in stand-up comedy. Watch a good stand-up act and notice how they switch topics. Try it—it's a lot of fun and makes you listen better too. When you realize that the current topic might kill the conversation, use it to segue towards something that won't. Also, if the conversation is moving towards a topic you don't know enough about, then either admit you don't know enough and ask questions, or find a way to move it in a direction where you can contribute while not diluting what the other person wants to say.

Basically, don't make it about you.

Because when you have a conversation with people with different knowledge bases and differing points of view, it's important to navigate it towards a satisfactory conclusion of mutual learning and evolution of your perspective as well as of those around you. That's the one reason why conversations matter as much as they do. They are mirrors held up to your evolving mindset and understanding of how you should move ahead in life.

Life Is a Series of Negotiations, Not a Competition

The ability to move others to exchange what they have for what we have is crucial to our survival and our happiness.
Daniel H. Pink, To Sell Is Human

'Hello, this is Duggi from AOL. How can I help you?'

'I want to cancel my AOL connection. I'm just not satisfied with it.'

'We're sad to hear that you're dissatisfied with our service. Is there anything I can help you with to resolve your dissatisfaction?'

'Nope, just cancel it. It doesn't work for me.'

'If there is any particular aspect of our service that has upset you, please rest assured that I'll be more than glad to help resolve it to your utmost satisfaction. We truly value you as a customer and would love to ensure you're satisfied with our service.'

Pause.

'You guys were doing a routine update to your connection in my house and my house caught fire. I couldn't call 911 because you blocked my telephone line while updating your fucking connection. Now my entire house burnt down and well, I guess your update must be done. So *no*, I don't think you can make a fucking satisfied customer out of me!'

Pause.

'I deeply apologize for everything that you have faced. Your account has been deactivated and you will get a confirmation on email shortly. Sorry for your discomfort.'

Click.

In the six months in 2005 that I spent working for the retention team at AOL, I gathered many experiences in negotiation and figuring out how to convince people to do something they didn't set out to do when they called. Our job was to retain customers who had called to cancel. And the range of issues people would dial in with was very broad and spanned from the pretty valid,

'I forgot when my free trial got over and I was suddenly charged!' to the instinctive,

'I don't like the sound your router makes.'

and sometimes, to the total facepalm,

'Your internet connection doesn't work.'

'Have you installed the connection properly?'

'What does that mean?'

'Have you inserted the disk you got into your CD drive to activate the connection?'

'That tray that comes out?'

'Yes.'

'I use that to keep my coffee mug. That's to put this thing in?'

On average, I received twenty-five to thirty calls every night (I was on the 2 a.m.–9 a.m. shift). Aside from the fact that this was one of the most harmful cycles for my health, it was the period that taught me how to instinctively gauge any situation and respond in seconds.

When you're on a call with someone thousands of miles away, you can't see them and their present situation in life. You need to analyse their state of mind in a few seconds to figure out how to make the sale. You need to have a quick-fire way to assess and respond. And over the first few weeks on the job, I instinctively built a system that helps me to this day.

People are as simple as they are complicated. We are defined by a few things:

- Where are we from? *(What's our daily life like?)*
- What's our ethnicity? *(What's our cultural conditioning?)*
- What's our emotional state? *(How are we feeling at a given moment?)*

It's these basic factors that define how people react and how they can be convinced, and I built a system around these basic tenets. When someone told me their name and where they were calling from, I had answers to the first two (my technique would change dramatically if someone was from middle America vis-à-vis either of the coasts, if they were Indian or Hispanic or Caucasian). But the third one was instinctive. It allowed me to both buy myself time to analyse their state of mind and keep them engaged. It was only years later, when I read the book *Never Split the Difference* by Chris Voss on the art of negotiation, that I found terms that explained the technique I had formed (and partially forgotten for a large part of my later years).

Reflecting Emotion with a Mirror

It starts with two techniques called 'mirroring' and 'labelling'. You mimic the other person's feeling, tone and mannerisms, and also repeat certain key words that they have used to get onto the same playing field and build a rapport or connection. It can be as simple as telling someone 'you sound upset' or 'you sound dissatisfied'. It's these small triggers that help hostage negotiators build a system of trust and understanding between them and terrorists. They help you understand what motivates an individual to behave and do the things they're doing in the moment.

> *Negotiation is not an act of battle; it's a process of discovery. The goal is to uncover as much information as possible.'*
> *Chris Voss, Never Split the Difference: Negotiating as If Your Life Depended on It*

Naturally, I wasn't playing with the same stakes as a hostage negotiator (I did get paid a bonus per successful call, and so it was crucial for me to get the other person to stay). So, I instinctively also understood the triggers that told me when to give up rather than keep trying. Because if I simply went ahead and booked a cancellation, the loss was just one customer, but if I stretched out a losing proposition, it wouldn't just be a failed call but also the probable loss of another successful call I could have done in that time.

That's what life is generally like. It gives you opportunities to gauge a situation, and you need to be able to analyse if that situation can be turned around to your advantage or you should just cut your losses and move on. It's by far the most critical thing I learnt in that period, and I've been trying to relearn it again over recent years. Not every situation can be won and not every person can be out-negotiated. Most of the time, it makes more sense to tell your ego that a loss was because of the situation, not you. Once you can learn to disassociate yourself in that, the choice becomes a whole lot clearer.

Happiness, Relationships and Love

Happiness, as it's said, is results minus expectations.
Morgan Housel, The Psychology of Money

There are some things we truly understand only in hindsight, and happiness tops the list. It is the end goal we all have in life. No matter what we want to achieve, no matter what we think we desire or what ambition drives us towards, in the end result we all seek happiness, to have that glowing feeling inside, that true smile on our face and warmth in our hearts. We all spend our lives looking for it but never truly understand it.

We also judge ourselves for finding it in arbitrary and frivolous things, in activities that seem unproductive and useless but which make us happy. We are too hard on ourselves and feel an overwhelming sense of guilt because we're watching too much Netflix or tweeting or scrolling away on Instagram or just letting YouTube autoplay videos infinitely on stuff like why the Harry Potter series is actually like *The Matrix* (look it up, it'll blow your mind). We are programmed to work, to focus on our career and productive growth, and to finally reach a point of independence so we can watch too much Netflix or tweet up a storm or scroll away on Instagram or just let YouTube autoplay videos infinitely on stuff like why the Harry Potter series is actually like *The Matrix* (seriously, you need to look this up).

Jenny Lawson in her hilarious and truly eye-opening book *Furiously Happy* puts it beautifully:

> You learn to appreciate the fact that what drives you is very different from what you're told should make you happy. You learn that it's okay to prefer your personal idea of heaven (live-tweeting zombie movies from under a blanket of kittens) rather than someone else's idea that fame/fortune/parties are the pinnacle we should all reach for. And there's something surprisingly freeing about that.

Once you realize that life isn't a sequence of work with an eventual pay-off of happiness, you learn to find happiness every day. There are micro-moments of happiness spread throughout our day that appear through life and pass us by as we keep building our life, and we often don't pause and let them truly soak in. Once I understood this, I learnt not to minimize those moments but truly work towards amplifying them. This doesn't demand that we lead a less productive life, but rather, it requires us to live a more optimized life. A life optimized for happiness.

Imagine that occasional walk you take on weekends with your music plugged into your ears. Why let it just be a weekend thing? Why not make it into an everyday habit? Perhaps it can be something you do with a friend, someone you love or just keep it as your time with yourself. Isn't that something to work towards, instead of aspiring and romanticizing the notion of not working at all one day and only then taking that walk on a beach all day every day? Why wait when you can have a tiny package of happiness now without compromising that future as well? Why not take micro-doses of the pay-off you eventually aspire to have? Happiness isn't an end result, it's a daily pit stop. The sooner we realize that, the better.

Take a ton of pictures, text your friends stupid things,
check in with old friends as often as possible, express
admiration to coworkers, and every day, tell as many people
as you can that you love them. A couple of minutes every
day—the payoff is small at first, and then it's immense.
Scott Galloway, The Algebra of Happiness

Happiness can be yours if you let yourself find and amplify the points in your daily life that bring you joy. And to amplify them, find someone to share those moments with you. There is no moment of happiness that doesn't become larger when you share it with someone you truly love.

The problem is that we often make it more about ourselves and lose the opportunity to share. Let me illustrate this with a physical exercise.

One Hand Trying to Clap

Have you ever tried to clap with one hand?

Seriously, try it! Put this book down, lift one hand and try to clap with it. Swing it in the air and see what you hear. That's what relationships are like if you don't value them—a mixture of empty air and you swinging your hand around with no one to tell you to stop being weird.

For a large part of my life, I was swinging my hand around and wondering why I couldn't hear any sound. I kept asking myself why I couldn't get the satisfaction of that nice burn you get on your hands with a solid clap of palms. I sucked at relationships, period!

And not just the romantic kind. Whether it was friendships, familial and beyond, I was constantly stuck on a 'me' cycle. It made me superficial at best when it came to forming bonds with the people around me.

What is a 'me' cycle, you ask? It's where you look at every action, every reaction, every favour, every conversation and every interaction and make it about yourself.

'It's all about me.'

'Let me tell you about me.'

'But what about me?'

'I understand your situation, but let's focus on me for a second.'

And I'm not the only one. As much as many of us don't want to admit it, we do have this mindset. We behave like this partly because of our insecurities and our fear of being judged. We also have a deep-seated worry of being omitted from the conversation if we stop bringing the focus back on ourselves.

For fear of feeling excluded, we don't let others feel included. Add to that the fact that the world we live in is, and has always been, focused on a constant stream of one-upmanship, on proving who's candy stick is bigger. We're also told to speak up, be leaders, make sure we top the class, run past the competition and pursue other such 'me over everyone else' ideals. So, we grow up thinking that the world needs to focus on 'me'. The sure-fire, fastest way to ruin any good relationship is to act, think and say, 'Can we just make it about me?'

And with me, it was all about 'me'. Every failed relationship would be a case of 'it's not you, it's me'. Every friendship not solidified, every meaningful connection not realized and every moment of hesitation to truly connect with someone was because of the 'me' cycle.

In many cases, this also stems from our environment we grow up in. Esther Wojcicki in her book *How to Raise Successful People* talks about Bowlby's theory of attachment, which 'suggests that the way we interacted with our parents when we were young will help determine our interpersonal relationships as adults, dramatically influencing the way we relate to other people, and most importantly to our partner and our own children'.

I'd like to build on this theory. It's not just how we interacted with our parents, but how we interacted with and learnt from the world around us as kids that determines how we consider relationships as adults. It's not all on the parents. I've understood this much better since I became a parent myself. Parenting is like an experiment you can never get fully right, no matter how much you try, because firstly, parents are human too, and secondly, they can't control the world and how their child interacts with it.

My parents gave me more opportunities to expand my mind and pick my options in life than most other kids my age had. And if you consider the fact that they were twenty and twenty-four when they had me, it's a miracle they figured out as much as they did. My parents always taught me to be myself, to open up to those around me, to be nice and not be too weird around others (I would insist on walking around in a Batman or Superman costume, so I can't really blame them). However, as I often say, 'No matter what you do, you will at some point take centre stage when your kid goes for therapy.'

So, in many ways, figuring out relationships is also a 'me' thing. It's driven by our personality and how we react to the world around us. That world has as much impact as our parents in moulding our mind and how we look at relationships and even love. It often makes us shy away from being vulnerable with someone else, and no relationship can be built through a wall.

It's easier to start a relationship with the door open than to pry open a door that's already been slammed shut.
Adam Grant, Originals

How do you pry open that wall? Find a way to peel away all the protective layers we've built around ourselves over the years to guard ourselves from being judged and getting hurt. And hurt is real, it's something we cannot deny. As we grow older, we form expectations from those around us, develop feelings that when left unreciprocated and unrealized leave us with an 'I can't go through this again, let's just wrap myself into a cocoon and not let anyone in' feeling.

In their book *Connect*, David Bradford and Carole Robin talk about the hallmarks of exceptional relationships. In such relationships, you are vulnerable and totally yourself (both of you), you can trust that anything you say won't be used against you, and you can settle conflicts in a productive manner even when you are being totally honest with each other. And most importantly, you are invested in each other's growth and development. Seems almost too good to be true, doesn't it? Like an ideal scenario you can put on paper? But is it even practically possible? The authors have an interesting solution for this as well, and they call it the '15% rule'. It goes something like this.

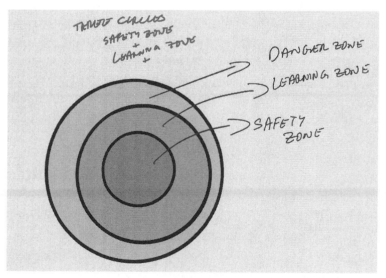

The Three Circles in a Relationship

Draw three concentric circles. The outermost one is your danger zone, filled with everything you would never consider sharing. The innermost one is your safety zone, which contains everything you would share without any worry. The middle circle is the zone of learning, through which you take something from the danger zone towards the safe zone. This middle zone plays a crucial part in the maturing of any relationship. It's where you start sharing things from behind your wall so that the other person can learn a little more about you. How you can build this as a process of sharing is the 15% rule.

Every time you're venturing into the learning zone, take a 15% step into it or a 15% step out of your safety or comfort zone. Gradually expand your safety zone, and when you start feeling uncomfortable, pull back 15%. Now, while the number 15 might seem arbitrary, it's basically a visual metric to ensure that you gradually open up, rather than take it too fast or too slow. Somehow, assigning a number to something keeps it quantifiable and measurable. In hindsight, when I look back at all my failed relationships, I either overcommitted too soon and opened up way too quickly, or never opened up enough to let the other person in. As with anything in life, it's the gradual steps that bring the highest dividends.

Then, as we share properly, we learn to listen properly, to be there for someone, to be as open to their emotions as we are to our own. And therein comes love.

Love is a tricky thing. We go looking for it in all the wrong places and read all the wrong theories of what it actually is. I blame many a movie for over-romanticizing the 'happily ever after' part of love. Over time, I have come to understand that it is actually at that point of 'happily ever after' that love truly begins.

I met my wife and the CEO of my life, Pooja, at a marketing conference. Chetan Bhagat (the bestselling author) was speaking, and I happened to spot Pooja as she spotted me. She gave me her visiting card in an extremely professional manner, and half an hour later, I asked her out for a drink (not too kosher a move in hindsight, but I thank my stars that I did). We met, we hung out, she went to America on holiday for a month, and we exchanged texts on WhatsApp constantly. All throughout, I was me (self-absorbed and clueless) and she was herself (clear-headed and mature). Her dog loved me (Tripp refused to stop humping my leg) and my friends called her my Everest (as in, I couldn't do better). In a couple of months we were engaged, then married and living together. Happily ever after, right?

What if I told you that over the last (almost) ten years, every year has come with its challenges and evolutions. Moments that have strained our relationship and yet eventually brought us closer together, moments when we learnt about each other, opened up about our feelings, our fears, our quandaries and our vulnerabilities. Over time, we discovered how to truly be ourselves with each other, and learnt to not just accept how we were deep inside but embrace the inner child in us. We learnt to complete each other in every possible way, to be able to travel the world together, to be silent in a room together doing different things yet be able to glance at each other and immediately draw out a smile. That, my friends, is love. It's a partnership built over time that's like fine wine—it gets better with time. All you need to do is open yourself up to it and invest in it. If it responds to you in kind, then you can have no greater happiness than to be with that person holding your hand.

This piece by Mari Andrew perfectly illustrates the feeling that is love.

I don't love you because you're the mythical 'right person'.
I love you because there are,
Things I want for you,
Things I want with you,
Things I want because of you.
Mostly I just want to stand beside you and go from there.

I Suck at Saying NO!
(How Do You Start Saying No?)

I just can't say 'no'.

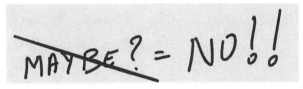

A Maybe Is Often a No in Denial

Most of the time, I would rather ghost someone or agree to do things I know I don't want to (or have zero inclination to do well) rather than try to muster the courage to say no. These options seem easier than being able to look someone in the eye and saying no! Simply writing this is sending shivers down my spine. At best, I might tell them no via text message, but even that takes a lot of willpower, and also, it is a terrible way to say no. It's a weakness I know I share with many of you.

I want to be liked. We all want to be liked. Even if someone says they don't care about being liked, chances are they care about it more than they say they do. We believe that everyone will like us because we're nice to them, and many a time, part of being nice seems to involve saying yes when your mind says no. Thanks to our need for social acceptance in a world that constantly believes in validation, we often worry about whether we should set boundaries and choose to shut the door on something or someone. What if they hold a grudge, or if it turns out to be a missed opportunity?

Let's tackle both of those one by one.

Jill asks Jack to accompany her to fetch a pail of water. Jack is swamped with work, and has neither the bandwidth nor the interest to do what Jill wants him to. But Jack is worried Jill may get upset if he says no, so he says yes. While helping Jill get the pail of water, he's distracted and is going over his to-do list on his phone. This lack of focus causes Jack to fall down and break his crown and Jill to come tumbling after, and the entire exercise becomes a failure. Jill is upset, Jack is hurt and the pail of water is empty. (I really need to move beyond nursery rhymes, but nothing else is universal enough, and anyway, they're much better than using X and Y).

What we don't realize is that often by saying yes, we do a disservice not just to ourselves but also to the other person. We live in a world overloaded with to-do lists, and a half-hearted yes will mostly deliver a substandard result. This will most likely eventually lead to a strained relationship between the parties concerned.

Now, if Jack had actually told Jill honestly that he didn't have the time to accompany her, or how he felt about it, things might have been better. Yes, she might have felt a little bad. But being honest and explaining the situation helps bring in clarity, and so when you actually do something for someone, it will be a genuine and focused effort. Besides, after Jack, Jill could have simply asked Humpty Dumpty to help her, since he would have been free after being put back together again (okay, I'll stop now).

In her book *Set Boundaries, Find Peace* Nedra Glover Tawwab writes about how a two-year-old can very clearly say no, but as that child gets older, adults start telling her that it's not nice to say no. Tawwab says, 'From a very young age, we're told that our boundaries are not nice or kind, and then as adults, we have issues setting boundaries.'

So, maybe it's time to embrace the essence of what that two-year-old understood (not literally, of course). Be mindful of how packed your schedule already is before you say yes to another task, or be true to your feelings and choose to say no. Frankly, if a relationship or equation can break because of a simple 'no', it wouldn't be a 'yes' in the long term anyway.

Next, let's look at the 'lost opportunity' problem.

We all have FOMO or fear of missing out, and it also drives our need to say yes to fleeting bright shiny objects. We are afraid that we might miss something good by saying no. Yes, in all probability there will be many things we say no to that will later turn out to be missed opportunities, stuff that would have been good to do. But every opportunity we take on shouldn't just be good, it should be great. It should be necessary and connected to your larger focuses in life at that moment. And it should add enough fuel to your long-term goals to fit into your time.

Ask yourself at every moment, 'Is this necessary?'
Marcus Aurelius, Meditations

Also, remember that if something doesn't fit into your scheme of things, then it's a no *for now*. It doesn't have to be a no forever. It's like the time I considered starting a YouTube channel or a second podcast. I had already been able to build my podcast following up to a certain scale, and I wanted to leverage that. But I knew that those additions didn't fit into my time and focuses at that moment. So, I said no to myself, till I eventually said 'yes' when I felt the time was right and it was essential for the next stage of my journey as a creator.

Our time is the most finite resource we have. So, if we don't say yes to too many good things, then we end up saving time to give to the one or two great things when they come along. Gauging what's good and what's great for us in the long term is the key to having a fulfilling life.

> Don't be on your deathbed someday, having squandered your one chance at life, full of regret because you pursued little distractions instead of big dreams.
> Derek Sivers, Anything You Want

Have a Stupid Chat

Not all conversations are meant to be meaningful. Not all of them have to necessarily drive some deep form of learning or value into our mind. There is value to what is called 'nothing', because nothing can be a lot of things. One of the greatest television shows of all time, *Seinfeld*, was famously called 'the show about nothing', because it was just the story of three normal people and their conversations about seemingly mundane things. But if it was about nothing, then why did it resonate so much with so many of us, and why do people watch reruns of the show even now?

That's because unlike the other shows at the time and those preceding it, *Seinfeld* showed us what most of our lives are like—normal. And normal isn't a bad thing. It's honestly what most of us secretly enjoy. We want a reasonably set routine, a weekend, hanging out with friends and the occasional vacation. Even the people hustling away to build something want to sell it for millions and then enjoy a set routine, a weekend, hanging out with friends and a vacation more often than usual.

That's where irrelevant and stupid conversations come in. We want to talk about random stuff, useless stuff, stuff that will make us laugh and banter and go to bed with a smile. Think about the last such random conversation you had with a friend, someone you've been friends with for ages. Someone who has known you long enough to not think twice before saying anything to you.

That just made you smile, didn't it?

That's the point. When we hang out with our closest friends, we don't discuss deep political, philosophical or economic topics. We talk about the time one of our friends called our professor 'mummy' by mistake (for the 10,00,000th time) and we still laugh about it. These scattered moments of nothingness and randomness drive and fill our hearts. They keep us emotionally secure and free of an 'agenda'. We can use all the mindfulness apps in the world, but nothing beats a random chat with an old friend.

These apparently mindless encounters are in many ways the secret to our mental health. Through such trivial discussions about superficial stuff with close friends, we actually open up to being ourselves. And that's the core of these conversations.

We spend a large part of our lives worried about perceptions, judgement and agendas. So, building deep friendships with a close set of people, with whom we feel safe enough to speak our mind and be stupid with, is the best investment we can make, both for ourselves and for them. In his book *Friendship in the Age of Loneliness*, Adam Smiley Poswolsky talks about the concept of 'deep hangs'. This is when we hang out with our closest friends without

My Boys/My Idiots

an eye on the clock (or on our phone), without the fear of being vulnerable. In such deep hangs, we attain what he calls a 'friendship flow state' that helps us blur out the world around us and focus on our time with them.

I've had the same set of closest friends since college. We catch up as often as we can, speak sporadically, take trips together and are always the same set of people when we meet. It's one of my most cherished treasures, one I depend on to cheer me up on my lowest and worst days. We all came to Mumbai as kids out of college and have never let the content of our conversations progress since. I'm often reminded of a line that Shah Rukh Khan tells Farhan Akhtar's character in the movie *Luck by Chance*, 'Don't forget those who were with you when you were nothing.'

I'd like to expand on that (sacrilege, I know) and say, 'Invest in your friendship with those who've known you and stuck with you since you were nothing.'

These guys mean the world to me. I've always wanted to put that on record, because they're idiots, but they're my idiots.

Leadership and Partnership: Two Sides of the Same Coin

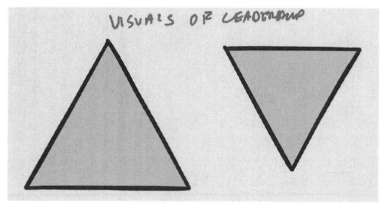

Visuals of Leadership

Look at the triangles above.

Take a pencil and highlight the triangle that signifies leadership to you. Try to not read ahead and choose; simply select the image(s) that signify the essence of leadership in your mind.

I'm asking you to do this because the pre-existent visuals in our mind are a great place to start if you want to understand what your perspective on leadership, and in turn partnership, is. It in turn can tell you what kind of leader or partner you might end up being.

So, close your eyes and visualize what leadership looks like to you.

If the visual you have is of a single person holding strings, a pyramid or triangle or the single person carrying everything, then you believe in the idolatry of the leader. You perceive a leader as someone to follow, to truly buy into his or her vision and believe in its gravitational pull. But if you visualized the line that connects the dots, the navigator with the telescope or the coach on the bench, then your perception of a leader is that of a mentor or a coach. And while this isn't a purely scientific way of understanding your perspective on leadership, it's a basic way to understand your mindset. It gives you a starting point as you set out to understand the kind of career and leadership journeys you can have.

There is a leadership methodology that I learnt from an interview by Guy Raz, the host of the 'How I Built This' podcast, of Marc Lore, the founder of Diapers.com (which was acquired by Amazon) and Jet.com (which was acquired by Walmart and eventually became the platform for Walmart to build their e-commerce business). He speaks of the 'mercenary vs missionary' mindset for leadership as a clear tracker of mapping someone's career journey, especially as a leader.

As the name suggests, a mercenary is a razor-focused, growth-driven leader. Someone who has a clear eye on growing the business and market share, and who drives shareholder value and bottom-line metrics. With a clear and pointed focus on a vision, the mercenary runs an almost authoritarian-style culture. The team is filled with sharks, wolf packs and personnel with such hunter-like qualities. Speed is paramount and so is winning at all costs.

On the other hand, the missionary drives a company through passion. She/he leads a team of individuals with a clear set of values and an obsession with contributing to something larger than just the bottom line. The missionary's mindset is that of a marathon, not a sprint, and so it's all about creating long-term value for the customers and employees of the organization, with a clear focus on not compromising the core values of the company.

The business space works largely with the mercenary mindset, but the world needs more missionaries. And that is where the tide is turning. Both employees and consumers today seek more than profitability. Authenticity, purpose and how a company truly affects the world around us are forming the foundation of the business world of the future. While we've got a long road to achieving this as a widespread way of working, it's never had as much momentum as it does now. And let me emphasize: companies with a missionary focus often create more value in more than one way by building a foundation of customer loyalty and a following for their purpose, all of which is definitely good for business.

So, where does that leave you? How does that affect the choices you make and the career you stitch for yourself as you navigate through the game of snakes and ladders that is the career-space? I'd say, start with ignorance and honesty and take it from there.

Out of the last fifteen years of my career, I've had the opportunity to lead in different forms for thirteen years. And I've always done it with ignorance, honesty and consciously surrounding myself with the smartest and nicest people ever. It's been a constant stream of figuring stuff out by asking and learning, trial and error, along with honing and refining my gut instinct. And the best way that I've been able to do this has been through partnership and shared ownership. Both of them are, to a large extent, the pillars of leadership. Let's start with shared ownership.

There is a simple fact all leaders, especially entrepreneurs, need to acknowledge: people at different levels of leadership have different levels of ownership. However passionate they might be, not everyone has as much at stake as you, the leader. Moreover, ownership often comes with equal weightage on bearing the brunt of the results if they don't go right, bringing a fear of failure into the mix. And that slows down progress in most cases. But does that mean you take control of everything and treat everyone like they have no ownership? No! The answer lies in moderation and balance, as Frances X. Frei and Anne Morriss write in their book *Unleashed*.

> Leaders must be intentional about distributing power and decision rights, and then take total, unqualified responsibility for the outcome.

This is something I've found to be supremely motivating in driving ownership and leadership. If all goes well, it's a collective win, but if all goes wrong, I bear the brunt, but ensure we do a deep dive into why.

I often use a plate of food as an analogy. We can only fit so much food onto our plate, so we need to shift some of that food to someone else's plate so you can add more to yours, until it fills up again and you repeat the cycle. That's how leadership works: you keep handing over responsibilities so you can add newer ones to your own, but you still hold the foundation of the plate. And the day you've handed over enough and aren't able to add more to yourself, you've successfully made yourself redundant, which I believe is the biggest validation of good leadership. That should always be your end goal. Having this mindset also keeps you level-headed and nullifies any god complex you might develop. Most importantly, it makes people feel valued for what they do and the perspectives they have. Stand back until you need to intervene, and always continue clapping from the sidelines.

> Even when people are well intentioned, they tend to overvalue their own contributions and undervalue those of others.
>
> Reid Hoffman

Balancing ego with ownership is the key. And your demeanour is even more important. If you stay calm during the storm, it will just feel like a strong breeze to everyone around you. Staying level-headed and forward-thinking in the worst and most stressful of times keeps everyone focused on what needs to be done, rather than what has happened in the past. Pessimism doesn't drive motivation, which is the primary force of leadership. If you feel pessimistic, learn to convert it into defensive pessimism. It's a process I've learnt over the years, and it wasn't until I came across this term in Adam Grant's book *Originals* that I found a name for what I had been doing since I was in school.

We all have self-doubt. It's natural. But if we let self-doubt drive our mindset, we'll never take a step forward. The trick is to not let self-doubt translate into fear, but rather, let it intensify our anxiety and then flip it around and use it as motivation. If we intensify the rush of 'Oh my god, this could go so wrong' and look at it from an 'I need to get this done so it doesn't go wrong' perspective, we will find the motivation to push onwards. It cautions us, and ensures that we don't become overconfident. It's actually one of the best methods when used properly (I also believe it's not for everyone unless they can naturally manage it).

But if motivation is your primary force, then where do you find yours? That's where partnership comes in.

There is an old saying, 'If your friend jumps into the well, it doesn't mean you must jump in too.' I beg to differ. If the 'right' friend jumps into the well, you jump along with him. I would not be where I am today if it wasn't for that one moment when Rohit and

Balancing Each Other

I quit our jobs to start The Glitch. And in many ways, I wouldn't be the person I am if it weren't for him. Partnership isn't just about moving towards a goal together. It's about sharing, balancing, driving and evolving one another. These four things make a partnership rock steady.

Rohit and I have always managed to balance each other out. Not by saying the same thing, but rather by saying different things that have been born out of the same belief system.

Shared beliefs simplify the world, because people who know what to expect from one another can act together to tame the world.

Jordan Peterson

Rohit and I believe in the same things, and so at a foundational level, we want the same things. Our difference in perspective always brought out the best in both of us. This simple fact allows partners to push each other to evolve, to not stagnate and to constantly challenge themselves to be better versions of themselves. Being aligned at a base level also makes being vulnerable easier. In my lowest times of self-doubt and failure, I've had someone with me who would give me a hug, a smack on the back and a terribly awkward joke that made me smile and find the will to move ahead.

That's also where trust comes from. When you can expose your vulnerable self and feel heard in return, when you never feel alone at your lowest and always push each other ahead, when you look at each other and understand things beyond words, that's when you build trust for life, and it's something that goes far beyond friendship and partnership. Trust is the bond that holds a partnership together. From the day we said, 'What's the worst that'll happen?' to the many failures and moments of glory, all that has mattered is that we've been able to share it with each other, laugh about it and take the next step forward.

Achievement is just a moment in pencil unless you can share it with people you care about. Then it becomes real, a memory in permanent ink.

Scott Galloway, The Algebra of Happiness

REFLECT

'THE INNER VOICE IN YOUR
HEAD IS AN ASSHOLE.'

Dan Harris

Learning to Be Self-Aware Is Like Learning to Breathe Underwater. It Takes Practice.

To be self-aware is often easier said than done. We mostly oscillate between overestimating what we can accomplish and underestimating what we are capable of.

When we veer towards overestimation, that's our ego telling us we can do something even though it's beyond us. We try to convince ourselves that we can wing it, that we know enough, that we're smart enough.

> Pride blunts the very instrument we need to own in order to succeed: our mind. Our ability to learn, to adapt, to be flexible, to build relationships, all of this is dulled by pride.
> Ryan Holiday, Ego Is the Enemy

We often blind ourselves to our own truth. We add terms like 'thought leader', 'subject matter expert' or 'motivational guru' to our bio without truly considering the depth and truth of these terms with regard to our own capabilities. I say this because those who truly are these labels emulate these words rather than use them as labels.

But ego aside, we often feel the pressure to project ourselves in a certain light, and over time, that doesn't bode well for our mental health.

When I think about the early days of starting The Glitch, I'm reminded of how little we knew and how much we winged it (winging it is still a constant feature in my life and how I go about doing things). I don't think this is just an entrepreneurial thing; it's how most of us navigate our careers. We reside in a constant state of overstating our knowledge and experience, and we're always stitching the parachute while we're jumping off a cliff. In fact, I remember a professor of mine once telling me that most people in the business world know only 10 per cent of what they claim to be their expertise.

On the other hand, I have to admit that there is a certain thrill to building something on the fly, creating a plan in motion and letting spontaneity drive sudden sparks of brilliance (in our minds at least).

But what we don't talk about enough is the anxiety and mental strain this puts on us because of the constant worry of being called out as a fraud or impostor.

And so, in flutters the 'impostor syndrome', constantly hovering at the back of our minds. It drives fear and insecurity into us, leading us away from risks and forcing us to do the exact opposite of our original 'you've got to run before you can walk' mindset.

Impostor syndrome (also known as impostor phenomenon, fraud syndrome or the impostor experience) is a psychological pattern in which an individual doubts their skills, talents or accomplishments, and has a persistent internalized fear of being exposed as a 'fraud'.

I harboured this feeling through a large part of my young adult life (even now, it pops into my head every so often). I veered between my ego and my insecurity—the former telling me I could accomplish any feat in academics or work or life without the effort, and the latter stopping me from asking any questions that might make me seem stupid. As a result, I constantly felt unsure and worried, and kept procrastinating for fear of falling flat on my face and someone turning around and accusing me of not being who I claimed to be.

It stuck with me throughout my early career, and I always veered towards options that felt safer. Why risk being a director and failing when I could be a producer and tread a safer path? (Little did I know that for a producer, the stakes are often higher.) Why claim to be creative when I could be the logistics guy who displayed flashes of creativity from time to time?

You tell yourself that you're closer than you think to what you want to do and end up risk-proofing yourself from failure or worse, like being called an impostor. The path you truly want to pursue often does seem to be the riskiest, but don't forget, it also promises the most satisfaction. Not because it makes you successful, but because it enables you to do what you truly want to do.

So, how do we flip the script on procrastination and the fear of being called a fraud, and bring our ego to the point of being honest with our true capability?

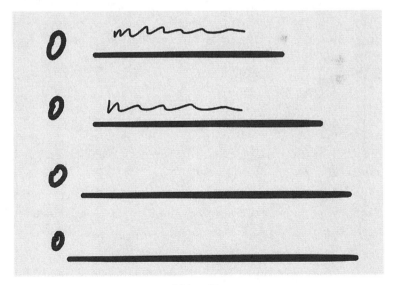

Make a List

For me, this changed when I learnt that I could turn this roadblock into the biggest driving force in my life. What if this very feeling of being an impostor could become my own personal superpower?

It required some reflection (actually, a lot), a bit of mental rewiring and building a framework of confidence for myself.

Let me tell you my process.

I started by making a list of things that I believed I knew a lot (or enough) about. These were things I thought I could do effectively, but in reality, I sucked at them.

Let's call this my personal 'fraud list'! And before we go ahead, you should put your own list down too. Don't just write bullet points, write the whole sentence. 'I'm actually very bad at managing teams and being structured in communicating my vision to them.' (That's one of mine, and it feels so satisfying to say it!)

You can write five, ten or whatever number suits you. Just make sure you're honest with yourself.

Then think about all the questions you have about each item on that list. Questions that you've wanted to ask but haven't for fear of being revealed as the impostor you are or of bruising your fragile ego.

List down the questions for each topic. Read them, tweak and improve them and read them again.

Now, jot down the things you are truly confident about. Again, be honest, tell that ego to calm down. This list—let's call it the 'confidence list'—contains things that you can do with very little hesitation or effort. Things you've done, practised and developed an almost reflexive skill set over your lifespan. For example, I can have a truly engaging conversation with almost anyone. Give me a topic and a person to start a dialogue with and I can take it from there. It might also be why I'm so comfortable being a podcast host, since many aspects of it are almost muscle memory for me.

Now take these two lists and put them next to each other. What you'll realize is that most of the things on your confidence list can help you improve the things on your fraud list. They provide the rope to pull them from the fraud side to the confident side. It's how I discovered that my lack of clarity wasn't an obstacle for the teams I worked with because it would often be nullified by my consistent conversations with them (rather than one-sided communication).

It's a slow process, but it will not only tell you what you could be a fraud at, but also what you are good at. And that flips your headspace towards a solution to the impostor syndrome. You can use the same ego-driven delusion that makes you overconfident and turn it into a system built for you to succeed.

However, always remember that the items from the fraud list can cross over to the confidence list only when you truly learn more about them.

The process helps you play to your strengths while giving your mind the ability to strengthen the weak areas in the shadows. It helps you ask the questions that matter, no matter how much you fear being judged because of them. It helps your fears and your strengths to work together to make you feel more whole and more secure.

> *Confidence is a measure of how much you believe in yourself. Evidence shows that's distinct from how much you believe in your methods. You can be confident in your ability to achieve a goal in the future while maintaining the humility to question whether you have the right tools in the present. That's the sweet spot of confidence.*
> *Adam Grant, Think Again*

Be Like Batman

It's not who I am underneath, but what I do that defines me.
Batman

I've always been fascinated by Batman. And not just for the obvious reasons. Of course, he's the coolest, there is no doubt about that. But there is something beyond that, something deeper that we can learn from and absorb into our own lives. Let me explain.

This is a guy with no superpowers. None! At some point, I'm sure we've all considered the fact that he must truly realize that he isn't actually qualified for the job (if he doesn't, then that's some next level denial)! While everyone else has superpowers, he only has a bunch of gadgets and a belt full of other stuff.

In spite of this, he's on equal footing with all the other superheroes most of the time. In fact, he's often the designated leader. It's pretty remarkable and mind-blowing when you think about it from that perspective. As I've dug deeper into this, I've always found that there is so much to be learnt from the phenomenon that is Batman.

I spoke about this a while back at a marketing conference and how this connects to what we should be as professionals and leaders, and I remember seeing a mixture of curiosity and bewilderment in my audience's eyes (it could also have been because my entire presentation was made up of memes, but that's not the point).

132

Why do we all love Batman so much, and more importantly, what can we learn from him?

Let's start with the fact that he's only human! He's burdened by all the things most of us are—our limited abilities, inner vulnerability, imperfections, our past experiences driving our present motivations and insecurities. All this encapsulates his truly human state of existence. That's what fascinates us and draws us towards him. Any of us can be Batman.

What has Batman achieved? He has understood his strengths and weaknesses clearly and worked towards getting himself onto an equal footing with the others. He's faced his faults and worked on them while accentuating his strengths. He's the kind who's realized that when life doesn't give you a level playing field, you hire a bulldozer and level it yourself.

He's built a niche for himself. He's the detective, the one who does his homework. Who creates opportunities and finds gaps that solve the mysteries no other superpower can. He's truly unique in what he does, and he knows it.

Batman knows the value he provides and makes sure he lets others know about it. We often undervalue ourselves or the role we play because we believe it might seem rude. Batman states the facts and the other superheroes respect him for that. Maybe we should too.

Let's admit it: not all of us are naturally gifted! But that doesn't mean we should sit on the sidelines and follow orders. In fact, a lack of natural talent allows us to look at the bigger picture more clearly! We're not focused on our strengths but rather on other people's weaknesses, especially our teammates, the talented ones.

And because he comes in with this mindset, Batman can assess all the other superheroes around him and figure out how they can work together and fill each other's gaps. That is what makes him a true leader. He can look at the macro picture and drive a set of talented individuals to focus on completing a seemingly impossible task.

Another specific skill that keeps him from getting too attached to every aspect of his goal is that he lets each of his colleagues do their thing. He knows that when a lot of people work together, each with ownership of a set of individual tasks suited to their strengths, they can achieve a larger combined goal. All Batman has to do is keep everyone of the path to success. This also allows him to let each of them take more credit than him for the things they've done. If that isn't leadership advice, then I don't know what is.

Finally, at no point does he move away from the reality of his innate 'humanness', or get carried away by the fantasy of the superhero. He always ensures that common sense prevails.

Everyone has limits they believe the world has defined for them. They choose to learn what these limits are and stay within the safer confines of not venturing beyond them. Batman chooses to treat these limits as things he can work around through the choices he makes, and by standing up to things beyond his reach of influence.

It's how I felt when I was first offered a podcast to host. Amit Doshi and Kavita Rajwade the co-founders of IVM Podcasts (one of India's foremost podcasting companies) offered me the opportunity to host a podcast on 'advertising, marketing and business'. And on instinct a large part of me was telling me to stay away and not risk it.

I had spent a large part of my life being a person who mumbled, who never portrayed clarity of thought in a streamlined fashion, who wasn't a definitive expert at anything. On that occasion, however, I chose to be Batman. I decided I could work on correcting my mumbling through practice, whereas my lack of streamlined thought made me a more natural conversationalist and my 'non-expert' tag allowed me to wear the learner's cap as a host. I told myself that I wouldn't stick to the range of choices I always picked from that helped me feel safe and within the confines of my limitations. I picked an option that presented itself to me and told myself that the experience would outweigh the risk of failure.

Don't Choose the Default

The choices we make in life help us decide who we can be. They also open us up to opportunities that seem out of reach, or seem to require skills or qualities that we have always considered to be our weak link. And no matter the situation, we control the choices that we make. And it's this ability to choose that no one can take away from us.

Consider who you are. Above all, a human being, carrying no greater power than your own reasoned choice, which oversees all other things, and is free from any other master.

Epictetus, Discourses 2.10.1

Being Fit for Life

'What's the point of those biceps if you can't carry a baby around for more than ten minutes?'

There are moments in our lives that are pivotal not just in our journeys but also in enabling us to choose a different and often better path. The moment when these words were said to me in 2018 transformed a part of my headspace. It was the space that had always looked at fitness as a means to an end.

At the time, the end was to make myself visually more appealing. Because let's face it, apart from sports, most of us don't really *want* to exercise, we're told we have to. Once we're told, our response is to grudgingly start some form of exercise. The problem with this is twofold: we feel forced into it, and the pay-off we're looking for isn't what we should be focusing on.

Let's consider a few statements to understand this better.

'Why don't you play a sport? It builds character! That's why I signed you up for tennis classes.'

'You spend too much time on the couch. Why don't you get out of the house and exercise?'

'You know it's just a month to go for our holiday, right? You might want to work on looking "beach ready"!'

'Did you hear about the guy who just ran a marathon but did it running backwards? We've got to try the normal way, at least!'

'*Evitandi paadepooyaru!*' Which translates from Telugu to English as 'Oh no, why have you gotten so spoilt!'

In most cases, the people who say these things mean well (except for the last one which I still haven't been able to figure out). But they don't understand the emotion they end up driving into our minds. We feel forced, shamed into submission, sold the virtues of fitness based on short-term, surface-level goals, and all of it to appease those around us. While a lot of these reasons can actually enable us to start, they often don't drive home the need to continue. Our reason for being fit lacks the core question most of us don't truly answer, 'Why do I want to be fit?'

It sounds simple, but it's often not focused on the 'I' but on everyone else. If the motivation to be fit doesn't come from within us, then any fitness activity we take up will never be long term, sustainable or genuine.

Before I go ahead, I know what you're thinking. 'Varun, why are we talking about fitness again?' And, 'Can you stop? You're making me feel exactly like what all those statements did.' So, before you move to another chapter or even put this book aside (don't you do that), I want to ask you one question.

What have you been unable to do in life because you just weren't fit enough for it?

It's a tough question. It isn't about what someone has said, but rather what you have been unable to do, even though you really wanted to do it. And that's the core reason why we should look at fitness from an inside-in perspective and not an outside-in one. We need to let what's inside us drive us to move and perform, not be pushed by some external force or validation. In doing so, we can dig deep in our mind and find our own sense of purpose.

But purpose doesn't come easy. I was a scrawny kid, constantly seeking ways to bulk up and get muscular because every action hero did. And while my parents never subjected me to any scrutiny, the world around did call me thin, lanky, scrawny or 'skin and bones'. I was told that I needed to bulk up to look better, and that validation drove me for years. It drove me in spurts and left me in droves. I tried everything from drinking raw eggs to changing gym after gym. All in search of that elusive, muscular, bulky me.

And then, years later, after I had finally managed to bulk up, grow muscles and got that sleeve looking tight around those arms, I heard these words, 'What's the point of those biceps if you can't carry a baby around for more than ten minutes?'

I'd just become a father and I couldn't keep up. I'd get tired after carrying our daughter around in my arms for ten or fifteen minutes, and even with the baby backpack, I would start huffing and puffing after carrying her for a few hundred metres. I had lower back pain, a shoulder rotor cuff strain, creaky knees, and I couldn't run more than a kilometre. I had just built the surface, but beneath it, I was hollow. That's when I asked myself, 'What was I unable to do because I wasn't fit enough for it?'

I realized that to be the kind of father I wanted to be, to truly be able to move in life as I got into my forties, I would have to recalibrate myself. I'd have to optimize for performance and not visual maintenance.

This holds true for all of us. We want to have enough energy to do everything we'd like to, we want to have the stamina to sustain that energy, we want to be balanced enough to be healthy and not constantly sick—in essence, we want to be fit for life. We should be able to run, jump and lift. We should be able to understand our own bodies to feed it right and build it well. We need to not lose the fun in our lives by overdoing diets and regimes, but find a way to balance all the fun with some structure.

We need to find the reason for being fit inside ourselves. We shouldn't rely on external drivers like being visually appealing for others or being able to show off washboard abs at the beach or just flaunting big biceps because all the famous people we follow seem to have them. These external or extrinsic drivers will be around only for a finite period of time. As our environment changes, so does the level of motivation we get from these external drivers. That's also the reason why we easily let go of our attempts at being fit. We let go if people around us keep coaxing us to eat healthy, or if we stop dating or if we're merely trying to look appealing to someone. If our drivers come from our environment, then we will forever be stuck relying on factors out of our control. And since those factors are ever-changing and inconsistent, our need to stay fit too doesn't last long.

Finding intrinsic or internal drivers that motivate us from within—like curiosity, passion and purpose—can help us find the ability to build systems we stick to in the long term. This is because internal drivers don't depend on anyone else, only our mind and body. This gives us more control over our own structures and how we function.

And there is another massive positive to this—mindset. As we learn how to optimize our bodies, we also teach ourselves how to optimize our mind. Therein lies the true value of being at peak performance. The positive mindset affects our entire system and gives us ways to perform, balance and optimize ourselves. It helps us achieve things that we once considered impossible. Because when we can build systems for ourselves, we can build systems for anyone and anything. If we find the motivation, it will drive us to learn, perform and eventually find a state of flow. As Steven Kotler says in his book *The Art of Impossible*, 'Motivation is what gets you into this game; learning is what helps you continue to play; creativity is how you steer; and flow is how you turbo-boost the results beyond all rational standards and reasonable expectations.'

So, list out the things you want to be able to do, and find your motivation deep inside you. You must have an area of your life in which you want to achieve something; learn as much as you can about that area by going down the rabbit hole that the world and the Internet have gifted you. Build your own personalized set of ideas and bring a unique and creative perspective to the table. In doing this, you can attain the ability to concentrate on the task you want to accomplish through a state of optimal performance, which is popularly called 'flow'. But remember, it all comes from within. You can start with a run outside not because the world wants you to or I'm telling you to, but because you want to get some sun and get in touch with yourself. You can motivate yourself to move ahead, keep taking that one step forward, and there is no bigger driver than that.

Rich Roll, the ultra-endurance athlete, author and podcaster puts it beautifully in his book *Finding Ultra* when he says, 'I didn't get into ultra-endurance sports to win races, beat others, or stand atop podiums. I got into it because it's a perfect template for self-discovery—a physical, mental, emotional, and spiritual odyssey to more deeply understand myself, determine my purpose, and discover my place in the world. A way to tap into my unexplored reservoirs of potential—and touch the other side.'

You Don't Need a Map to Find Joy

Life is full of possibilities. You just need to know where to look.
Joe Gardner, in the movie Soul

Joy Isn't as Distant as You Think

We focus a lot on purpose as a key driver in our lives. As a way to define ourselves. And I've never really been able to put my finger on what my 'purpose' is. I've tried to do everything, from reading about defining purpose, finding frameworks, attending courses and workshops to even a brief attempt at looking inwards for purpose during my therapy sessions. But there was always a voice from within me that said:

'Do you really need to?'

'Does it have to be only one?'

'If there's more than one, does one become primary and the others secondary?'

It wasn't until I watched the movie *Soul* one evening in August 2021 that I found a way to resolve this quandary. Without getting into any spoilers (and infringing any copyrights), I must say that the movie solidified a belief I've had in my mind for a while, which is that the purpose of life is to live.

We don't soak in all that life has to offer. We've closed our senses—eyes, ears, tongue, heart and mind—to things we find mundane, regular and small.

Instead, we go seeking the new. It's our instinct to look for new, greener and bigger pastures, to find solutions to all our ambitions, problems and gaps. But most of the time, the true answer to these lies in the things and moments we take for granted, in the forgotten and the old. Every once in a while, we should revisit, rejuvenate and reboot elements that were once at the core of our life, but that have slipped into the background and been taken for granted over time.

Early in my entrepreneurial journey, I had set myself a goal of retiring by the time I was forty-five. I was going to start the clichéd bar on the beach. I began working so hard and with such focus that every holiday, experience and moment was overshadowed by my purpose of building the company we had set out to build, and always giving it the priority it needed so I could truly 'live life' later.

I was fortunate that I married someone who showed me the value of balance, breaks, experiences and moments. I remember Pooja telling me on our first holiday together that I should try to switch off my phone, stay away from my emails and just soak in the world around me. She wanted me to truly taste every morsel of food, enjoy every walk, every sight, sound and everything else that stimulated my senses.

I slowly began to realize that true living comes from being able to balance life and career so that both can bring deep satisfaction. And while I am thankful for the privileged position the results of my work has brought me, I also know the effort it has taken for me to unplug, to live the moment and to not only work hard and party hard but to work smart and live well.

I achieved this by learning to think of joy and happiness as breadcrumbs scattered around us. We need to not just follow them but also consume them with the same enthusiasm we would give to any life-changing or purpose-driven task. The one big moment of joy shouldn't be our end goal, but rather, finding joy in our everyday life.

The other day, I went for a run on the top of our apartment building in Mumbai, and instead of listening to a podcast or audiobook, I decided to run in silence. I looked at the world around me, felt the breeze on my face, smelt the moisture in the air and saw the beauty in this loud, messy city I call home. It made me smile, and I ran longer than I intended to.

To think I'd lived there for two years and only experienced this now is a reflection of our times. Life is meant to be lived and experienced—that's our purpose and that's what our soul truly wants. The day we realize this our eyes will truly open to what life has to offer. In her book *Joyful*, Ingrid Fetell Lee speaks of this, 'Joy's power is that small moments can spark big changes. A whimsical outfit might prompt a smile, which inspires a chance kindness toward a stranger, which helps someone who is struggling to get through her day. Even the tiniest joyful gestures add up over time, and before we know it, we have not just a few happier people but a truly joyful world.'

I like to think of those moments as tiny initiators of joy. They are things, places, rituals and moments that, despite being repetitive, give us that feeling of peace and happiness (not necessarily in that order) to truly enjoy what life has to offer. Joy doesn't have to come from deep meaningful places; even the silliest and most routine things can lead to the most joy-filled moments in life. So, don't forget to look down and spot the breadcrumbs every day, to watch the sunset, sip on that cup of tea, message your sister, listen to that song, remind yourself to soak in the mundane moments that you've taken for granted because they might bring you more joy than you can imagine.

Tiny Moments of Happiness

Nothing in life is as important as you think it is when you are thinking about it.
Daniel Kahneman, Thinking, Fast and Slow

'I found her. She's throwing up. I think she sneaked in some pizza last night! You have to get here, everyone's freaking out!'

I woke up, rubbed my eyes and checked my watch. It was 4.45 p.m. and I'd only managed to get two hours of sleep). I splashed water on my face, popped some toothpaste in there and left my room.

'Okay, I know you need to shoot the sunset set-up at 6 p.m. but it's not going to be ready before 8. So, we're definitely going to miss the sunset. People are tired, man. It's been mad!'

Right. Another crisis to attend to, but first, pizza.

This was 2008. I was working on my first large-scale project as a producer, a model hunt reality show called 'Get Gorgeous'. The guy who was supposed to actually produce it quit a month before shooting began, and the channel was out of options. So, they decided to let a couple of us 'assistant' producers take on the show.

We jumped at the chance, and it was chaos from day one. Delays, mishaps, behind-the-scenes drama, plus a set of celebrities that refused to behave like decent human beings. But, as I'd realize later, this was pretty much every reality TV set.

145

On day two, those two problems cropped up. I headed to the room of one of the contestants who'd thrown up after eating pizza (they were on a cleansing diet and her body had rejected the damn thing). I hadn't slept in a week and looked like death. The two hours I'd just gotten was the most I'd slept in the previous forty-eight hours. That's when I noticed something.

In the middle of all of this madness and people running around, one dude was sitting on a lounge chair looking out at the beach. It was Vikrant, one of the camera guys taking a break in between the chaos. He saw me looking at him and waved me over. I was pretty cheesed off but curious too, so I walked over.

'What's up dude?! Come, sit down!'

'Uh, no man. I have a lot of stuff to deal with.'

'Come on, just sit! Here, take this glass of beer and just look there for five minutes.'

I looked to where he was pointing and paused. It was like everything had suddenly slowed down and all the noise had been drowned out. I sat down, took the glass he offered me and kept looking.

What lay in front of my eyes was beautiful. The sun was just starting to hit the sea and the waves were at just the right height as they hit the beach. I was in Kerala, and the scene in front of me was something people come all the way from across the world to see. I closed my eyes, took a deep breath and soaked in the breeze as the sound of the waves touched my ears and the warmth of the setting sun caressed my face. I smiled after what felt like ages.

He saw my face and said softly, 'What's the point in doing what we do if we don't get to enjoy this, man? Take a second once in a while. That's what makes it worth it.'

My smile widened to a grin. What he said made sense. There's no point in doing what we do in life if we don't get to soak in the sun and feel the breeze every once in a while.

I've had many moments of far larger significance in my life. Moments of magnitude, of resounding celebration, happiness and accomplishment. But when I set out to think of a story to explain the significance of tiny moments of joy, this one kept coming up.

That might seem odd. I certainly thought it was, but as I reflected further, it made sense. When you think about it, our lives are made up of tiny moments of clarity. Moments of emotion, reflection, revelation, stillness and randomness that are markers in the journey of our lives. They don't alter the course of our lives, but in many ways, they help refine the evolution of our character.

Brené Brown in her book *Daringly Great* puts this beautifully, 'Joy comes to us in moments—ordinary moments. We risk missing out on joy when we get busy chasing down the extraordinary.'

There is so much truth in this. Although we look at larger goals and glorious ambitions, true satisfaction comes in the smallest fragments of our lives. It's during these times when we as individuals move in a certain direction, initiate a personal system or habit, or just kick off what becomes a lifelong passion or endeavour.

These moments also help us take a pause and look around, look back and look ahead. But most importantly, they tell us to look at where we are now and help us make the most important decisions of our lives.

And looking back at my time while I was writing this book, it wasn't the big stuff that kept occurring to me. I kept thinking of stories, moments or incidents to distil down the learnings I've gathered through my early twenties, during my tryst with reality TV and my time as an entrepreneur who, over the last twelve years, has grown a tiny creative company from his living room to (arguably) one of the largest creative agencies in the country. But it wasn't the big wins or the celebrations or the growth or our acquisition by the largest creative network in the world that popped up. What popped up were conversations, tiny moments of reflection or just single, sometimes weird, instances.

And they turned up again when I thought about my journey in life and as a husband and a father. Everything initially seemed arguably tiny and inconsequential, but somehow, the more I looked back at them, reflected and digested their hidden insights, the more their importance grew in my mind. Because all our lives are normal, and what makes them unique are these moments.

It's an exercise I wish I'd done sooner in life. It's something most of us fear or forget to do, but what we don't realize is that at worst, they might make you smile, and at best help you gain a deeper insight into your life. And I think most of us would settle for the smile.

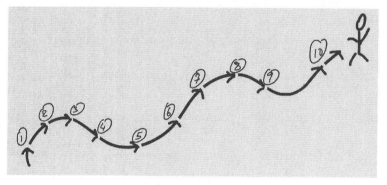

Ten Moments in Life

So, at this moment, if I asked you to pick ten instances or moments of learning from your life, no matter their significance or magnitude, what would they be? Take a piece of paper and scribble the first five, ten, twenty that come to mind and then cross off any you want to (or just keep all of them, there are no rules for this). Leave that paper alone and come back to it after a few hours or days, depending on your ability to resist your FOMO.

When you come back to your list, you'll realize that most of them aren't the biggest moments in your life, are they? Instead, they're tiny instances that seem to have had such a profound impact on you that they've stayed embedded in your mind. Like tiny footnotes that help you fill in the gaps that were conveniently left out of the stuff 'you need to know to navigate and survive life'.

While life doesn't come with an instruction manual, it does come with its fair share of moments that are like loose pages of that manual. Those pages are scattered all around while life happens around you. All you need to do is simply pick them up.

Bibliography

Start

The Big Leap: Conquer Your Hidden Fear and Take Life to the Next Level by Gay Hendricks, Harper Collins Publishers India Limited, 2014.

Range: Why Generalists Triumph in a Specialized World by David Epstein, Macmillan, 2020.

The Multi-Hyphen Method: The Sunday Times by Emma Gannon, Hodder Paperbacks, 2019.

Justin Timberlake's quote from *Two Beats Ahead: What Musical Minds Teach Us About Innovation* by Panos A. Panay and R. Michael Hendrix, Penguin Business, 2021.

Derek Sivers and Tim Ferris's quote from *Tools of Titans: The Tactics, Routines and Habits of Billionaires, Icons and World-Class Performers* by Tim Ferris, Random House, 2016.

The Book of Moods: How I Turned My Worst Emotions into My Best Life by Lauren Martin, Grand Central Publishing, 2020.

My Inner Sky: On Embracing Day, Night, and All the Times in Between by Mari Andrew, Penguin Books, 2021.

Quentin Tarantino from *The Joe Rogan Podcast*.

Dream With Your Eyes Open: An Entrepreneurial Journey by Ronnie Screwvala, Rupa Publication India, 2016.

Choose

Greenlights by Matthew McConaughey, Headline Publishing, 2020.

Grit: Why Passion and Resilience Are the Secrets to Success by Angela Duckworth, Vermilion, 2017.

'Furiously Happy': A Funny Book about Horrible Things by Jenny Lawson, Picador, 2016.

Keep Going: 10 Ways to Stay Creative In Good Times and Bad by Austin Kleon, Workman Publishing, 2019.

Learn

The Socrates Express: In Search of Life Lessons from Dead Philosophers by Eric Werner, Simon & Schuster, 2020.

Made to Stick: Why Some Ideas Take Hold and Others Come Unstuck by Chip Heath and Dan Heath, RHUK, 2008.

Steal Like an Artist: 10 Things Nobody Told You about Being Creative by Austin Kleon, Adams Media, 2014.

Atomic Habits: An Easy and Proven Way to Build Good Habits and Break Bad Ones by James Clear, Random House Business Books, 2018.

Talking to Strangers: What We Should Know about the People We Don't Know by Malcolm Gladwell, Allen Lane, 2019.

The Ride of a Lifetime: Lessons in Creative Leadership from 15 Years as CEO of the Walt Disney Company by Robert Iger, Bantam Press, 2019.

The Death of Expertise: The Campaign against Established Knowledge and Why it Matters by Tom Nichols, OUP USA, 2019.

Excerpts from Al Pacino's speech from *Any Given Sunday* (Warner Bros) in *Greenlights* by Matthew McConaughey, Headline Publishing, 2020.

Drunk: How We Sipped, Danced, and Stumbled Our Way to Civilization by Edward Slingerland, Little, Brown Spark, 2021.

Get Out of My Head: Inspiration for Overthinkers in an Anxious World by Meredith Arthur, Running Press Adult, 2020.
Stillness Is the Key: An Ancient Strategy for Modern Life by Ryan Holiday, Profile Books, 2019.
Two Beats Ahead: What Musical Minds Teach Us about Innovation by Panos A. Panay and R. Michael Hendrix, Penguin Business, 2021.

Connect

Think Again: The Power of Knowing What You Don't Know by Adam Grant, WH Allen, 2021.
To Sell Is Human: The Surprising Truth about Persuading, Convincing, and Influencing Others by Daniel H. Pink, Canongate Books, 2018.
Never Split the Difference: Negotiating as If Your Life Depended on It by Chris Voss, Random House Business, 2017.
The Psychology of Money by Morgan Housel, Jaico Publishing House, 2020.
'Furiously Happy': A Funny Book about Horrible Things by Jenny Lawson, Picador, 2016.
The Algebra of Happiness: The Pursuit of Success, Love and What It All Means by Scott Galloway, Bantam Press, 2019.
How to Raise Successful People: Simple Lessons for Radical Results by Esther Wojcicki, Hutchinson, 2019.
Originals: How Non-conformists Change the World by Adam Grant, Viking, 2016.
Connect: Building Exceptional Relationships with Family, Friends and Colleagues by David Bradford and Carole Robin, Penguin Life, 2021.
Set Boundaries, Find Peace: A Guide to Reclaiming Yourself by Nedra Glover Tawwab, Piatkus, 2021.
Anything You Want: 40 Lessons for a New Kind of Entrepreneur by Derek Sivers, Penguin, 2015.

Meditations by Marcus Aurelius, Modern Library, 2003.

Excerpt from Shah Rukh Khan's dialogue in *Luck by Chance* (Excel Entertainment).

Marc Lore's quote from the podcast *How I Built This* with Guy Raz.

Unleashed: The Unapologetic Leader's Guide to Empowering Everyone Around You by Frances Frei and Anne Morriss, Harvard Business Review Press, 2020.

Reflect

Ego Is the Enemy: The Fight to Master Our Greatest Opponent by Ryan Holiday, Profile Books Limited, 2016.

Think Again: The Power of Knowing What You Don't Know by Adam Grant, WH Allen, 2021.

Discourses 2.10.1 by Epictetus, Penguin Classics, 2008.

Finding Ultra, Revised and Updated Edition: Rejecting Middle Age, Becoming One of the World's Fittest Men, and Discovering Myself by Rich Roll, Harmony, 2013.

The Art of Impossible: A Peak Performance Primer by Steven Kotler, Harper Wave, 2021.

Excerpt from Joe Gardner's dialogue from *Soul* (Pixar/Disney).

Joyful: The Surprising Power of Ordinary Things to Create Extraordinary Happiness by Ingrid Fetell Lee, Rider, 2018.

Thinking, Fast and Slow by Daniel Kahneman, Penguin, 2012.

Daring Greatly: How the Courage to Be Vulnerable Transforms the Way We Live, Love, Parent, and Lead by Brene Brown, Penguin Life, 2015.

Acknowledgements

When I set out to write this book, I didn't realize what a journey of highs and lows it would be. Over the last year, I've had periods of stasis, anxiety and confusion. I've gone through days of not being able to write anything. Weeks where I wasn't sure what this book would even come together as. And days when I almost gave up. And in these periods of shutdown, I've had many a person who's come to my rescue. To help clear my mind, give it structure and help pull me out of the mindset and mood that was clouding what I was looking to put down on paper. And I want to acknowledge and thank everyone who helped me.

Firstly, my biggest strength, my voice of reason and clarity, my wife, Pooja. She's the reason I got through this year with a semblance of sanity and with a book in hand. She breathes clarity into my muddled mind and holds fort while I scream 'catastrophe'. Mostly, she can calm the need for drama deep within me by smacking some sense into my head. This book is what it is because she never let me question myself, and for that (and for most things in my life today), I say this book has been held together by her, as is my life.

To my parents, for patiently letting me be a curious, indecisive, often painful and yet entertaining kid for the last forty years. You let me explore what my mind and heart desired, and I am what I am because of that.

To Shreya, my commissioning editor from Penguin, for always giving me a sense of clear direction amid every storm, writing block, deadline extension and late-night brainwave. You've held the spine together on this one. (And thank you to Nikhil Taneja for helping start this entire journey that has been the best creative experience in my life. I owe you one.)

To Vijay Subramanium for reminding me over many a late-night call why I was writing this book in the first place and ensuring I keep my eyes on the prize.

Among all the people whose writing has inspired not just what I've written but rather how I've written this book, no one stands out more than Ryan Holiday. His notecard system helped me find a way to put a disjoined series of ideas into one free-flowing book, and his daily stoic reminders kept my mind and soul at ease.

To everyone who's consumed any piece of content I've put out and reacted to it. Thank you for helping me try and understand what resonates and interests you. This book contains many ideas and concepts that I've seen audiences connect with in my podcasts, newsletters and beyond. You've helped me understand you and, through that, my own mindset.

And lastly, but most importantly, I want to thank the kids in my life—Megha, Leia, Lulu and Tripp. One is the world's best sister, another the daughter who keeps my heart warm; the other two, the canines, have the love of the world in them. You make me want to be better for you every day.

(And to those of you who've read the book and come this far, thank you! I hope you found stuff that made you smile, introspect, reach clarity or just pause to think for a second. If you've folded the corner of a few pages and highlighted a few lines, then I consider my job done. Thank you for reading something I've dreamt of writing for as long as I can remember.)